M000201604

Julie has beautifully captured the spiritual and emotional ups and downs of the adoption journey. I encourage all prospective adoptive parents, and those in the midst of their journey of parenting kids from hard places, to read this book. You'll be encouraged and refreshed as you press on in your calling.

KELLY ROSATI
Vice President of Community Outreach, Focus on the Family

Julie's book is a great guide for future adoptive parents as well as a guide for parents who are questioning their motivations for adopting. The book makes us aware that adoptive families are the true heroes for orphaned and vulnerable children.

BILL BLACQUIERE
President and CEO, Bethany Christian Services

I loved *A Call to Love*: It's the book I always planned to write one day! It's biblical, educational, practical, and comprehensive. There is so much in here that captures my own experiences as the parent of a child adopted from foster care—and what so many of my former clients experienced when I was a social worker—as well as what I know remains true today as I engage in domestic and international advocacy for children.

CHUCK JOHNSON
President and CEO, National Council For Adoption

A CALL TO LOVE

A CALL
TO LOVE

*Preparing Your Heart & Soul
for Adoption*

JULIE HOLMQUIST

TYNDALE HOUSE PUBLISHERS, INC.
CAROL STREAM, ILLINOIS

FOCUS ON THE FAMILY® | FOCUS ON PARENTING™

A Call to Love: Preparing Your Heart and Soul for Adoption
© 2018 by Julie Holmquist. All rights reserved.

A Focus on the Family book published by Tyndale House Publishers, Inc., Carol Stream, Illinois 60188

Focus on the Family and the accompanying logo and design are federally registered trademarks of Focus on the Family, 8605 Explorer Drive, Colorado Springs, CO 80920.

TYNDALE and Tyndale's quill logo are registered trademarks of Tyndale House Publishers, Inc.

No part of this publication may be reproduced, stored in a retrieval system, or transmitted in any form or by any means—electronic, mechanical, photocopy, recording, or otherwise—without prior written permission of Focus on the Family.

All Scripture quotations, unless otherwise marked, are from *The Holy Bible, English Standard Version.* Copyright © 2001 by CrosswayBibles, a publishing ministry of Good News Publishers. Used by permission. All rights reserved. Scripture quotations marked (AMP) are taken from the Amplified® Bible [paraphrase], copyright © 2015 by The Lockman Foundation. Used by permission. (www.Lockman .org). Scripture quotations marked (NASB) are taken from the *New American Standard Bible.*® Copyright © 1960, 1962, 1963, 1968, 1971, 1972, 1973, 1975, 1977, 1995 by The Lockman Foundation. Used by permission. (www.Lockman.org). Scripture quotations marked (NIV) are taken from the *Holy Bible, New International Version,*® *NIV.*® Copyright © 1973, 1978, 1984, 2011 by Biblica, Inc.® Used by permission of Zondervan. All rights reserved worldwide. (*www.zondervan.com*). The "NIV" and "New International Version" are trademarks registered in the United States Patent and Trademark Office by Biblica, Inc.® Scripture quotations marked (NKJV) are taken from the *New King James Version.*® Copyright © 1982 by Thomas Nelson, Inc. Used by permission. All rights reserved. Scripture quotations marked (TLB) are taken from *The Living Bible* [paraphrase], copyright © 1971 by Tyndale House Foundation. Used by permission of Tyndale House Publishers, Inc., Carol Stream, Illinois 60188. All rights reserved. Scripture quotation from *The Message* copyright © 1993, 1994, 1995, 1996, 2000, 2001, 2002 by Eugene H. Peterson. Used by permission of NavPress. All rights reserved. Represented by Tyndale House Publishers, Inc.

People's names and certain details of their stories have been changed to protect the privacy of the individuals involved. However, the facts of what happened and the underlying principles have been conveyed as accurately as possible.

The use of material from or references to various websites does not imply endorsement of those sites in their entirety. Availability of websites and pages is subject to change without notice.

Cover design by Libby Dykstra

Cover photograph of girl and teddy bear copyright © Westend61/Getty Images. All rights reserved.

For information about special discounts for bulk purchases, please contact Tyndale House Publishers at csresponse@tyndale.com, or call 1-800-323-9400.

Library of Congress Cataloging-in-Publication Data can be found at www.loc.gov.

ISBN 978-1-58997-940-6

Printed in the United States of America

24	23	22	21	20	19	18
7	6	5	4	3	2	1

To my children Anna, Ben, and Masha—
I'm so glad God gave me the privilege of being your mother!
Being part of your lives is a precious gift, and I can't imagine life without you.
And in honor of my son Daniel Timothy Holmquist
(Born Anatoliy Kozhevnikov in Novozybkov, Bryansk, Russia)

Contents

Foreword

No two adoptions are quite alike, each with all the distinctive curves and contours of a fingerprint. But almost every adoptive parent I know shares similar words about the journey: "Some of the hardest things I've experienced. The most meaningful, too." Isn't that true of nearly all the best things this side of heaven?

The truth is, if we've never uttered words like that, we probably won't have much to look back on in the end. But when they're threaded deep into the cloth of our days and years, those words yield a life well worth living.

So adoption has everything to do with what we desire most.

If things like comfort, convenience, and smooth sailing top our wish lists, we'll likely want to steer clear of adoption (and perhaps of just about *any* worthwhile endeavor).

But if we value other things even more—things like the rough-and-tumble of life in a family . . . the way parenthood can double the capacity of our hearts and then double it again . . . the chance to be menders in a torn world . . . moments in which our lives humbly reflect the way God first loved us—then adopting may very well be one of the best and most significant decisions we ever make.

I remember vividly the days when I first began to ponder that choice. My wife was ready for the adventure, already a couple of steps ahead. But in my head, all the excitement and hesitations were having a massive tug-of-war.

It made for quite a ruckus inside. And amidst it all came the weight of countless questions starting with "How": *How do we even begin weighing all the options and counting the costs? How can we prepare for a journey that is certain to stretch us in every way, from our finances to our marriage? How do we answer questions we don't even know to ask?*

That's where this book comes in. *A Call to Love* is the kind of guide I wish I'd had when we started grappling with these questions and many others. I trust I wouldn't have decided differently, but it all would have been with a much fuller sense of what I was embracing . . . and how to do so wisely and well.

Yes, I'm one of the many who've said these words, at times with knitted brow and set jaw, more often with a grin and laughter in my eyes: "Some of the hardest things I've experienced. The most meaningful, too."

I hope these realities will prove true for you as well, because they almost always come together. And when you really think about it—especially in moments when you ponder what kind of life you want to look back on from the end—isn't that what you want too?

Jedd Medefind
PRESIDENT, CHRISTIAN ALLIANCE FOR ORPHANS

Introduction: The Journey to Adoption

Whoever receives one such child
in my name receives me.

MATTHEW 18:5

One year my husband surprised me with a hot-air balloon ride as a Mother's Day present. I still remember five-year-old Ben and six-year-old Anna watching from the ground as their mother floated up into the heavens. Little did I know then, as I soared above the Saint Croix River valley in Wisconsin where we lived, that my family wasn't complete.

I didn't know that someday I'd be flying to Russia to unite with two preteens who had stolen my heart. I didn't know they'd give me a ride that would bring me much closer to heaven—and God—than any giant hot-air balloon could. But God knew. In 2002, He began whispering *adoption* to my spirit.

Perhaps God has also whispered to you, and you are beginning to listen. You might be exploring, unsure of where God is leading you. Maybe you know beyond a shadow of a doubt that God has called you into the ministry of adoption, and you want to know what to expect.

No matter where you are in this process, I invite you to learn from others as they describe the emotional and spiritual landscape of adoption. If you've already made the decision to adopt, you can also record your unique spiritual journey within these pages.

Remember that you are not alone. As you travel through a process that can be incredibly joyful one day and deeply painful the next, know that God is with you each step of the way. He has promised to "never leave you nor forsake you" (Hebrews 13:5). In fact, you may find that this journey will lead you to a closer, deeper relationship with your heavenly Father.

Many people have walked this road before you, and you'll hear about some of their journeys in this book. Some struggled to choose adoption after facing infertility. Others were hesitant to obey what God had called them to do. Most battled fears. Would they be able to love the children they adopted? Would they have enough money? Would they be adequate for this task? Would they be able to handle any "issues" their children had?

And once they made the decision, the process instigated doubts. Could they truly trust God to choose a child for them? Would they be able to deal with the foster-care system? Would the wait ever end? I understand, because my husband and I asked those same questions.

As you begin your own journey to adoption, I'm praying you'll be encouraged as you read how God reassured and directed other couples. Their stories also reveal how God uses the process of adoption to grow people's faith and deepen their trust in the Father who adopts all of us as His children. He will do the same for you if you keep turning to Him.

My family's journey began one morning as I read John 14:18 during my devotion time: "I will not leave you as orphans; I will come to you." I'd read this verse many times, but this time the Lord was giving me a command, speaking deep into my heart.

Don't leave them as orphans, Julie. Go to them.

Eventually, that's what my husband and I did. We adopted

Daniel (eleven) and Masha (ten) on June 2, 2004, in a Russian courthouse and brought them home to join our two biological children, Anna (fourteen) and Ben (twelve).

While your journey will be different from mine and every other story within these pages, there is really only one narrative here. It's the story of God's love for orphans and for us.

Just remember, God's adoption of us as His children was not without cost. He gave His only Son, who suffered for us. If your role in God's story includes adopting a child, it's likely that your journey will involve difficulty and struggle too. Being a loving parent of any child—biological or not—involves sacrifice, dying to self, and suffering, as well as incomparable joy. Yet the difficulties can often be magnified when we adopt children, simply because they have already suffered at least one loss—or, most likely, multiple losses and trauma—before arriving at their new homes.

I remember that when my husband and I were praying about adoption and reading descriptions of wounded children in the US foster-care system, I saw a picture of Jesus while browsing through a store's craft section. This phrase accompanied His image: "I didn't say it would be easy. I said it would be worth it." I knew it was a message for me.

I've learned from numerous adoptive parents, and from my own experience, that the cost of adopting a child can also bring unexpected joys. One of those joys is a chance to know Christ and His astounding unconditional love at a deeper level as we attempt to model that love for our new children.

As you listen to the stories within these pages, ask your Father in heaven for His thoughts. My prayer is that God will direct you as you prayerfully consider your role in His story and the next step in your adoption journey.

PART 1

Making Decisions

CHAPTER 1

Great Expectations

A wonderful gift may not be wrapped as you expect.

JONATHAN LOCKWOOD HUIE
100 Secrets for Living a Life You Love

"Go ahead, kick me out!" bellowed my son in that serious Russian voice of his as he jumped up from the kitchen table. "Why did you even bring me here? I don't belong here!"

My family of six was having a noisy dinner at the time. Everyone was talking, and I had apparently missed something Daniel was trying to say to me. He took this as a sign of rejection—he took most everything as a sign of rejection. I knew what he was thinking: *It's better to leave first, before they get rid of me. Because it's just a matter of time before they abandon me, just like Mom and Dad did.*

It had been seven months since my husband, Jeff, and I had adopted this boy and his eleven-year-old sister, Masha, from a Russian orphanage. In our hearts and minds, they were officially

Holmquists, joining our teenage biological children, Anna and Ben. But Daniel didn't believe he could actually be part of our family. Assuming this sensitive, hurt boy would immediately trust us was expecting too much.

Our new son had communicated his distrust for months in the strange ways that only a traumatized, anxiety-ridden English-language learner could. That January evening in 2005, he expressed his fear of being abandoned by letting the front door bang shut behind him and running into the darkness.

"Daniel! Come back!" I called out to him. "I just didn't hear you. You *do* belong here!"

I ran after him—down our snow-covered rural Wisconsin driveway, down the road lined with pine trees—breathing in air that pierced my lungs like icicles.

"It's too cold, Daniel. You can't run away in your socks!" I shouted in typical mom fashion, as if common sense would make a difference.

I barely got the words out as I quickened my stride. I was forty-two and not an athlete, yet here I was chasing down a preteen who could run circles around me. I came close enough to snag my son's sweater, but he simply took it off, leaving me standing there incredulous, the sweater hanging limp from my fingers, my breath visible in the night air.

There was just enough moonlight for me to see Daniel's barechested, thin body as he stumbled on, arms flailing. He was crying and moaning with a depth of sorrow I couldn't comprehend. The cold air on his chest must have impeded him, because with a final burst of speed, I was able to grab my son and wrestle him into the snowy ditch. Slowly I led him back to the house—he'd given up the fight. I was shaking with exhaustion as I looked to the clear, cold sky.

I'm too old for this, Lord! I'm just way too old for this.

My lungs ached from the freezing air. My body hurt and my soul was frightened. What if Daniel would never trust me?

This wasn't a scene I'd expected as my husband and I began preparing for adoption in 2002. What had I expected? Nothing, I thought. I wasn't looking for new children to fulfill my dreams. After all, I'd already given birth to Anna and Ben, and Jeff and I had experienced many storybook—and stressful—parenting moments. For fourteen years I'd enjoyed the special fun of loving and raising a boy and a girl. My house had seen its share of Tonka trucks, Barbie dolls, birthday parties, ear infections, Lyme disease, and surgeries. No, I didn't believe I was taking anything for granted. I wasn't wishing for children with any particular qualities as my husband and I obeyed what the Lord had called us to do.

In hindsight, I realize that I *did* have expectations. I expected our new children to trust us. For Daniel, who had been deeply hurt by every adult he had ever loved, developing that confidence in us took more than a year. I'd also assumed I'd have another daughter who liked to talk a lot and share all of her feelings with her mother, but I was wrong. I expected all of my children to become instant best buddies since they were so close in age. I didn't consider how major personality differences, emotional-maturity gaps, and living with a traumatized sibling would affect these relationships. I expected our love and knowledge as parents to heal every wound our new children might have. I wish I could tell you that this expectation was fulfilled, but it wasn't.

I'm not the only adoptive parent who has been taken by surprise. I'm sure the couple who adopted a neglected, abused two-year-old boy hadn't expected his first words to his new father to be "F— you!" And the parents who had provided the foster-care system with a long list of criteria for a child didn't expect God to say, "Do you trust Me to choose the child?"

As the mother of biological children who are now in their twenties, I can tell you that surprises and unmet expectations are the norm for all the children we raise. Life throws all of us more than a few curveballs, and that brings us to the next point.

EXPECT THE UNEXPECTED

It's not news that our expectations and reality often collide. That perfect job requires us to work with (surprise!) imperfect people. After moving into the house of our dreams, we discover cracks in the foundation, noisy neighbors, or an unpleasant, recurring odor from a manufacturing plant located miles away. When we welcome children into our lives, we may dream of what those baby boys or girls may become, but God has a way of showing us that our children are uniquely created in His image, not according to the fantasies in our minds.

Why does a couple initially mourn when their child is born with a disability? Because their expectations of having a healthy newborn weren't met. Why does a father feel a loss when his son isn't interested in his favorite sport? Because his expectation of enjoying football with his boy wasn't fulfilled.

It's important to realize up front what your assumptions about adoption may be, because they will affect how you treat and respond to your new child, as well as the health of your marriage and even your relationship with God. If you're considering adoption, ask yourself, "What are we expecting from this?"

Hopes of buying frilly little-girl dresses or providing a perfect playmate for an only child shouldn't be foremost in your mind as you approach this journey. I like frilly girl dresses myself, so I enjoyed buying one in anticipation of my daughter Masha's arrival. But I'll never forget the look on her face during that first week in our house after she donned the dress for church.

I asked the college student interpreting for us that week to ask

Masha if she liked the dress. The Russian-speaking student translated my daughter's words as "Yes, I like it," but Masha's body language was clear. She hated this horrible, flouncy thing! Her expression was the same as Ralphie's when he was forced to wear the pink bunny suit in *A Christmas Story*. As soon as I realized how she truly felt, I took her by the hand to her room, showing her with my actions that she could wear something else. That frilly dress disappeared, and we've often laughed about that day.

Of course you'll be excited about bringing home a new daughter or son; just don't set yourself up for disappointment by expecting all of your dreams to come true. The girl you adopt may not only hate dresses but may also seem to hate *you* as she hurls all the pain and rage of her considerable losses your way. The child you may already have at home and your new child might have completely different interests and be jealous of each other. The kid you pictured following in your footsteps as an academic whiz may need special education at school.

Adopting a child won't solve your problems, fix marriage difficulties, or magically dispel that grief you feel because of infertility. In fact, adopting a child is likely to add stress to your life, just as caring for a newborn does. While adoption will certainly allow you to love, care for, enjoy, and raise a child—your child—expecting this little boy or girl to heal your inner wounds, erase your disappointment with God, or mend a relationship is clearly unreasonable. Though you may know all this, you may long for an easy solution and create one in the recesses of your mind.

If you're married, consider how you felt during the honeymoon period. When we fall in love with our spouses, we often think irrationally. I know I did! I thought Jeff could do no wrong, that he was perfect. I expected him to make me happy all the time, to solve all of my problems, and to basically be

God! After I surrendered my life to Christ, I realized what I had unconsciously required of my husband. Only God can fill the role we sometimes unwittingly grant to spouses and children.

When Kimberley Raunikar Taylor and her husband adopted their first child (a toddler) after years of infertility, they decided to keep expectations low.

"Preparing our hearts and minds to accept the absolute worst scenario in an adoption situation helped us to not place false expectations on our adoption," writes Taylor in her book *The Intentional Family: Celebrating Adoption*. "So when the trials came, we were not shocked and were more able to cope with the situation. Conversely, when the blessings came, we were more able to appreciate them as well."[1]

During the first year with their son, Taylor reports that she and her husband were "challenged more emotionally, physically, and spiritually than we had ever encountered in our lives. But gradually, things got better."[2]

EXPECT STRONG EMOTIONS

Along with unexpected situations come unexpected emotions, both wonderful and terrifying, and your responses, both positive and negative. There may be the sky-high joy of holding your child for the first time and bringing him or her home after a lengthy adoption process, as well as the deep satisfaction of meeting a neglected child's needs.

Like Jeff and me, you may experience the peace of knowing you're doing what God has called you to do, the total delight of recognizing your son's sense of humor, or the surprising feeling when that intense protective feeling for your daughter kicks in for the first time.

We discovered Masha's and Daniel's senses of humor immediately. The adoption agency we used flew orphans to the United

States for "visits"; it was a way to fulfill Russia's adoption regulation requiring prospective parents and children to meet on two separate trips.

On the first day of this monthlong visit in our home, my husband explained the house rules to Masha and Daniel (Anatoliy at the time). One was "Laugh a lot." Before we knew it, Daniel was making funny faces as he stood behind the couch, acting as if someone were pulling him down. Masha loved transforming her face with generous amounts of cellophane tape, making her nose look snout-like. My husband joined in the slapstick, and by the end of the month, Daniel had declared, "Papa goofy!"

There may also be times of intense despair as you try to bond with your child, when you're weary of trying to connect to a little girl or boy who desperately wants to cling to you one minute and then rejects you the next. Maybe, like me, you'll find a child's constant challenging behaviors toward you so provoking that you lose your temper and throw a phone against the wall, then later find yourself overwhelmed with shame and hopelessness because of your reactions.

Clinical social worker Sharon Roszia explains that children who have experienced trauma speak about their past through behavior:

> The child's strong, reactive emotions, based on that early trauma, are "catchy" and can quickly create trauma in the family. . . . Having parented traumatized children myself, I know that the child's feelings of helplessness, avoidance, isolation, and rage are easily triggered in the new family. I remember such a moment when I was enraged with one of our children. I glanced at myself in the hallway mirror and saw the face of a raging shrew staring back at me! I had never met that part of myself before.[3]

If you're hit by strong negative emotions, use that as a cue to take a break. Then ask God for self-control and understanding about what's happening in your child's spirit and in your own. Seeking professional advice can bring needed clarity into these relationship dynamics.

EXPECT TO HELP YOUR BIRTH CHILDREN

If you already have children at home, realize they will also need time to adjust to a new sibling and will need your help to do so. Jeff and I discussed the idea of adoption with Anna and Ben and asked them to pray about it. Though they agreed to move ahead with the adoption and were willing to share their bedrooms, they certainly couldn't imagine what life would be like with two younger kids permanently in the house. Suddenly Anna and Ben didn't have their parents to themselves. Masha and Daniel were not only loud and noisy but also broke some of Anna's and Ben's belongings. Home life definitely changed for my two oldest children!

Let your biological kids know that adjusting might be hard and will take time. Don't expect them to bond immediately with your new child, but consider ways you can promote connection between the kids. You might assign common jobs or projects they can do together, or have your children teach the newcomer how to treat a pet or play a favorite game.

Make sure to schedule regular alone time with your biological children, no matter how much time and energy your new child demands. It's easy to become overwhelmed and not do this; I know because it happened to us, and we regret it. Your birth children need your help to process the changes of a different family structure and any trauma behaviors your new child might display. I remember my fourteen-year-old daughter crawling onto my lap during those early days, seeking security from her mom who was suddenly so busy with two other little people.

Your birth children need some "normal" time with their parents—just you and them. This gives them a break from the new family dynamics. Ask them how they're doing, listen to them, and validate their feelings. Take any actions needed to assure them of your love.

EXPECT A DEEPER JOY

Many times, hard-won victories for you and your new child will follow a moment of despair, and that will produce a deeper kind of joy. That January night when Daniel ran from our house (as he had many times before) was one of those moments for me. I could have given into doubt as I often had during the recurring stressful situations of our first year together, but on this particular evening, I was able to choose hope instead.

After I lugged this dark-eyed, handsome boy through our front door, I put my arms around him. I knew I needed to show him—once again—that I loved him. After he finally started to relax, I led him to our secondhand rocker-recliner, and I rocked this twelve-year-old like a baby. I told him (again) that I loved him. I assured him (again) that I would never leave him. I reminded him (again) that I would always be his mom. This calmed and reassured him (again) that his new parents weren't going to send him back to Russia. After almost a year of mothering him, Daniel was able to tell me, "Mom, I'm beginning to believe you."

You can also expect a deeper joy as you seek God during the adoption process and move closer to His heart. James 4:8 says, "Draw near to God, and he will draw near to you." It seems as if God uses our earthly adoptions to communicate to us in profound ways.

This was the case for pastor and author Francis Chan after he and his wife decided to adopt a girl they were fostering. The joy came, Chan said, when he heard from God as he spoke to his soon-to-be daughter.

After a social worker asked how long the foster girl could stay in his home, Chan said he looked into the girl's eyes and told her, "Honey, don't worry; you can stay here as long as you like. You can be one of my daughters. Do you see how I treat my daughters? You can be one of them. I see you as my girl. Everything I have is yours."

At the same time, Chan felt God saying, *Francis, don't you see that this is what I say to you? Why do you still sometimes have a hard time believing that? Why do you think you—as a human being—can look at this girl and say, "Everything that's mine is yours; I'll take you as my own"? Do you not believe that I've said that to you?*

Chan says he had a childhood that left him feeling insecure, but in that moment God reminded him—His adopted son— that he was completely secure in God's love and provision. "It was one of those moments in my life where I just felt like God was reassuring me," Chan reflected.[4]

While no one can be prepared for every possibility as a parent, life may be less traumatic for you and your family if, as a couple, you examine your expectations of adoption. The One who created you and knows your inmost being is able to reveal any unreasonable assumptions you may have about adopting a child, so pray separately as well as together about the issue. Ask God to show you how to approach adoption in a healthy way. Doing this can help you draw closer to the Lord as you seek to discern how He wants to use you and your family to care for orphans.

And remember, the unexpected things in life can be beautiful. As a kid, Masha didn't care for frilly dresses, but she could clean a bathroom until it shined (every mother's dream!), and she liked poetry. Both were welcome surprises. Letting go of unrealistic expectations allows you to focus on who your child really is and what he or she really needs.

Rest Stop

1. As you examine your expectations for adoption, ask the Lord to examine you. "Examine me, O LORD, and try me; test my mind and my heart" (Psalm 26:2, NASB).

2. Write a list of expectations you may have for a child. Then consider Lamentations 3:24: "'The LORD is my portion,' says my soul, 'therefore I will hope in him.'" As you pray for a child, are you placing your hope—or expectation—in God alone?

    Think about one of your hopes for a child and insert it into the last part of this lamentation. For example, "Therefore I will hope in *having a boy who loves baseball*." After you list all your expectations, strike a line through them, replacing them with "Therefore, I will hope *in God alone*."

    Pray together as a couple, surrendering your lists to the Lord. Ask God to align your expectations with the child He has chosen for you.

3. Begin your journal on the next page.

My Journey to Adoption

DATE _____

Learn to love without condition. Talk without bad
intention. Give without any reason. And most of
all, care for people without any expectation.

Unknown

CHAPTER 2

Reality Show: Infertility

*Participate joyfully in the sorrows of the world. We cannot cure
the world of sorrows, but we can choose to live in joy.*

JOSEPH CAMPBELL
A Joseph Campbell Companion

"If we want to have more children, we can always adopt," my
husband said as we scheduled his vasectomy in 1992.

Back then we weren't living our lives for the Lord, so we certainly didn't ask God for His opinion on the matter. We assumed
adoption was something simple, just another way to fill our
needs if we chose to enlarge our family later on. I imagine I was
too busy being sleep deprived and changing the diapers of two
babies (one who was sick most of his first year) to give adoption
much thought.

If you and your spouse haven't been able to conceive, you
would probably like to throttle us right now for choosing that
operation. I don't blame you! After I surrendered my life to
Christ, I grieved this decision that should have involved Him.

If you long to have biological children but cannot, you're well acquainted with a deep grief. In *Spoken from the Heart*, former First Lady Laura Bush describes what you already know: "For those who deeply want children and are denied them, those missing babies hover like silent, ephemeral shadows over their lives. Who can describe the feel of a tiny hand that is never held?"[1]

The drive to procreate is an ancient force, a desire reflecting how we are made in the image of a creative God, a Father himself. Even though I had already given birth twice, I still longed to have another baby only two years after my husband's procedure. But it hit me that this was now impossible, and there was grief in that. I cannot imagine the grief of infertility.

After I prayed about my desire, I was asked to serve in the infant nursery for a two-hour church event. The ratio was ten to one—I was the one, and the ten were the babies who cried, needed diapers changed, and wanted to be held. Too many babies and not enough me! I was exhausted by the time the mothers returned and interpreted this experience as a message from God.

Okay, Lord, I told Him, *maybe I won't be having any more babies.*

In the end, it was God who decided the next steps for expanding our family: He told us to adopt, He chose the children in answer to our prayers (we were initially thinking of adopting one child, not two siblings), and He even made the route clear for us. All we had to do was obey.

"We don't have enough money for international adoption," my husband had said as we discussed our options. We earned about $55,000 a year as owners of a weekly newspaper in rural Wisconsin.

"And there are kids right here who need us," I added. "Besides, children in foster care speak English, so we wouldn't have to worry about a foreign language."

But as you already know, God pointed us in a different direction. After waiting about six months to be matched with an older child through the foster-care system and having no success, we received a simple phone call that led to Daniel and Masha coming into our lives. We knew they were God's choice.

I could see God chuckling as He made our path clear. These siblings lived halfway around the world, and the only English they knew was Masha's handful of words (*Mama* and *Papa*) and Daniel's few classroom sentences: "This is the yellow monkey" and "Good morning, teacher."

WHY ME?

As you've probably already discovered, trying to understand God's ways is impossible for mere humans. But still we try.

Sheridan Voysey, who with his wife, Merryn, tried to conceive for ten years without success, wanted desperately to understand why God hadn't given them a baby. Maybe, he thought, he was doing something wrong.

"Perhaps I didn't pray enough, exercise faith enough, oppose the devil enough. . . . Feelings of spiritual failure haunt me," he writes in his book *Resurrection Year*.[2]

If you're wondering why infertility had to knock on your door, consider the story of Zechariah and his wife, Elizabeth, in Luke 1. Their story illustrates a truth we don't talk much about, says Pastor Josh Lindstrom of Woodmen Valley Chapel in Colorado Springs, Colorado. "Faithfulness," he states, "does not guarantee the absence of disappointment."[3]

Zechariah had been a faithful priest his entire life, and his wife was a righteous woman from the line of Aaron, so hers was a priestly, godly heritage. Yet they were childless most of their lives, an incredible disgrace in that culture. They had done nothing wrong; Elizabeth's barrenness was not a punishment. Then when they least expected it, when their bodies were too old to conceive, God worked a miracle and gave them a very special son—John the Baptist.

You might be thinking, *Sure, they had their miracle. But where is ours?* You may be as righteous as Zechariah and Elizabeth, but you're still dealing with disappointment.

Philip Yancey, who has never fathered children, shares this helpful viewpoint:

> I've talked to many people over the years who will have one thing that they wish was different. They might say, "I wish I was married," or "I wish I had children," or "I wish I *didn't* have children." I don't find a lot of help in dwelling on things that can't change. We seem fascinated by cause—why did this happen? The Bible doesn't really give us a lot of help on the issue of cause. In fact, it tends to switch the focus to our response: Now that it has happened, what are you going to do about it?[4]

YOUR RESPONSE

One way to respond to your situation is to get right with God before adopting a child, especially if you still harbor emotions about infertility that could become destructive.

Some (but definitely not all) husbands or wives who've dealt with infertility may find themselves mired in bitterness and envy, says Dr. Russell Moore, president of the Ethics and Religious Liberty Commission of the Southern Baptist Convention.

After his wife suffered three miscarriages, Moore says he found himself bitter toward God. He advises those seeking adoption to first take stock of their spiritual state through prayer and advice from godly friends and pastors.

Moore and his wife, Maria, later went on to adopt two boys.

Eventually, they also had biological children. Just don't count on adoption as a cure for infertility, Moore warns. "If you're thinking about adoption as a way of bargaining with God, as though he'll repay you for your adoption with 'kids of my own' later, then put adoption aside. Your potential children need parents—not to be a pawn in someone's attempt to manipulate the Almighty."[5]

Uncovering and dealing with any unhealthy motives for adopting is of major importance, according to the late Dr. Karyn Purvis, cofounder of the Karyn Purvis Institute of Child Development. Parents must be focused on the needs of the child, not their own.

"That little person in front of me doesn't have capacity to meet my need. And if I come to him expecting him . . . to, I've already set [him] up to fail," Purvis said in a radio interview. "We say to parents, 'Yes, if God's called you and your spouse to do this [adopt], that's glorious. Make sure it's His timing.'"[6]

As with all else in the Christian life, getting right with God means bowing to His will and surrendering to His sovereignty, even if that means accepting circumstances and limitations we don't understand, don't want, or find heartbreaking.

Psalm 31:14-15 says, "I trust in you, O LORD; I say, 'You are my God.' My times are in your hand." It doesn't say, "I trust in You, Lord, but only if You give me what I want." That sentence seems audacious in print, but isn't it true that we can easily think this way?

Yet Jesus tells us, "If anyone would come after me, let him deny himself and take up his cross and follow me. For whoever would save his life will lose it, but whoever loses his life for my sake will find it" (Matthew 16:24-25). If we're following Jesus, we must continually surrender our wills, our lives, and our bodies to Him. The apostle Paul, who himself had a physical ailment that God chose not to heal, urges us in Romans 12:1 to offer our bodies as "a living sacrifice, holy and acceptable to God," in an act of worship.

As you offer your body to God just as it is, remember its great worth. Because if you have believed that Jesus Christ is your Lord and Savior, your body is the temple of God! Whether or not your body can produce physical offspring, God's Holy Spirit dwells in you (1 Corinthians 3:16). Your body is akin to the Old Testament's ark of the covenant, where God chose to manifest His presence and glory. With Him indwelling you, you can produce spiritual fruit of great worth.

WISE CHOICES

The late Ann Kiemel Anderson, a bestselling author who had multiple miscarriages and later went on to adopt four boys with her husband, realized she had a choice as she faced heartbreaking losses. "I could make sorrow my friend or my enemy. Sorrow could make me hard and cold and bitter . . . or sorrow could be my best friend and teach me things I had never known before. I reached out and took sorrow's hand."[7]

As you seek to let go of any bitterness or anger that may keep you locked in the past, and as you surrender to God in your circumstances, consider what He may have for you in the future. Isaiah 43:16, 18-19 says,

> This is what the LORD says—
>> he who made a way through the sea,
>> a path through the mighty waters, . . .
> "Forget the former things;
>> do not dwell on the past.
> See, I am doing a new thing!
>> Now it springs up; do you not perceive it?
> I am making a way in the wilderness
>> and streams in the wasteland." (NIV)

God did a new thing in the lives of David Platt and his wife, Heather. Platt, a pastor and an author, writes that God used "this hardship [infertility] in our lives to lead us to adopt a precious little boy in an obscure city of northwestern Kazakhstan whom we would never have met otherwise."[8] After the adoption, Heather quickly became pregnant, and the couple eventually welcomed two biological children. Even so, they both wanted to adopt another child.

"We are forever grateful for the five long years of infertility that God led us through," Platt reflects. "God had opened our eyes to the needs of the orphan, and an adoption process that began as a desire to fill a void in our hearts became a desire to reflect a reality in God's."[9]

(✏) Rest Stop

If you need a refresher course on the absolute sovereignty of God, read God's response to Job in Job 38–41. God didn't give Job a reason for his immense suffering. He didn't explain why. Instead, He reminded Job that He—the Creator of all things—was in complete control of the universe. If you need to surrender your why to the Lord, ask Him to help you do so. As you consider your response to infertility, record your thoughts on the journal page.

My Journey to Adoption

DATE _____

We know that for those who love God all things work together
for good, for those who are called according to his purpose.

Romans 8:28

CHAPTER 3

Reality Show:
Wounded Children

Oh, lift me as a wave, a leaf, a cloud!
I fall upon the thorns of life! I bleed!

PERCY BYSSHE SHELLEY
"Ode to the West Wind"

When my husband and I began the adoption process in 2002, I discovered how wrong we were when we had flippantly remarked, "We can always adopt." My research revealed that adopting through the foster-care system wasn't a simple process.

Part of that process involved attending classes so we could become licensed foster-care parents. That's when God showed us in great detail that this adoption was all about the needs of the child He would send our way. We would be required to make sacrifices to meet this child's needs, and in fact, we would need to absorb a child's pain. To make sure we understood His message, God surrounded us with several studies of the book of Job—in our church and on the radio.

Adopting a child can certainly expand your family in a beautiful way and allow you the joy of parenting a boy or a girl for the first time. But as you envision a pink bedroom or a toddler bed sporting a comforter decorated with cars, you must also prepare yourself for another reality: the need to nurture a wounded child.

Many children in the foster-care system have suffered trauma, and now research has shown that even otherwise healthy infants feel the traumatic loss of their birth mothers.

"Only a small percentage of children [in the United States] are orphaned at birth," reports Jedd Medefind, president of the Christian Alliance For Orphans. "As a result, the majority of kids currently available for adoption are . . . older, have special needs, or are part of sibling groups. When families adopt without preparing for what might be required to heal a wounded child, it is a recipe for heartache."[5]

ADOPTION STATISTICS

- Number of US children adopted in 2014: 110,373[1]
- Number of US infants adopted in 2014: 18,329[2]
- Number of US children adopted from foster care: about 50,000 per year from 2002–2014[3]
- Average age of a child waiting to be adopted: 7.6 years old[4]

NOT A FAIRY TALE

"In the United States, . . . children end up in foster care due to founded allegations of abuse or neglect in the homes in which they're being raised," says Kathy Ledesma, the national project director of AdoptUSKids.[6] According to Harvard University data released in 2005, children in the US foster-care system experience trauma in the form of post-traumatic stress disorder (PTSD) at a rate more than twice that of combat veterans.[7]

For many children with tough beginnings, developing close relationships with their new parents often takes time and is a messy, hard business. According to Dr. Karyn Purvis, author of *The Connected Child*, about 80 percent of children who experience abuse, neglect, and/or trauma "are disorganized in their attachment style," which means the child doesn't know how to make relationship connections. If a child has an attachment issue, Purvis observed, "The big challenge is that all the messages they give you are counterintuitive to what they really want. . . . They desperately want a relationship, but they don't know how to do it."[8]

Daniel Bennett, adoptive father and author of *A Passion for the Fatherless*, points out that "orphan care ministry is not a fairy tale. It is a God-glorifying tragedy. No matter how wonderful it is to care for a child who is an orphan, we cannot escape the tragedy that began the story. God will be glorified through the story and [parents] will experience joy," he adds, but they must not be blind to possible difficulties.[9]

SEVEN CORE ISSUES

So how do you face reality as you begin your adoption journey? Educating yourself is a good first step, one you've already begun by reading this book. You'll want to learn not only about the common inner wounds children can have when they've lost their biological parents or have been neglected or abused, but also about parenting strategies that promote healing.

Social workers Deborah Silverstein and Sharon Kaplan-Roszia identified seven lifelong or core issues in adoption so people would understand that being adopted is *different* from growing up in a family of origin. Those core issues are

- loss,
- rejection (abandonment),
- guilt/shame,
- grief,
- identity,
- intimacy (relationships), and
- mastery/control.[10]

As an adoptive parent, I can tell you that I've seen these core issues play out in my home and many other adoptive parents' homes to one extent or another. You can read about them at the Child Welfare Information Gateway.[11]

It's not hard to see how an older child who has experienced neglect, abuse, and abandonment is wounded. It's less intuitive to understand how children adopted at birth could be affected by loss—but they don't have an easy out either. Their senses were attuned to their birth mothers, even in utero. Just because they can't speak doesn't mean they haven't been hurt.

"Even if the loss is beyond conscious awareness, recognition, or vocabulary, it affects the adoptee on a very profound level," write Silverstein and Kaplan.[12]

This statement is now backed up by neuroscience and brain-imaging research, which has exploded since the 1990s and has shown us how the brain reacts to—and is changed by—early trauma.

When we consider how a child's relationship with his or her mother begins in the womb, we can begin to grasp the depth of such a loss. According to Dr. Karyn Purvis,

> Baby's heartbeat beats to mama's heartbeat. The baby moves hands and feet to mother's voice when mother's talking. . . . They [baby and mother] come into synchrony, and neurochemically they match by six months in utero. . . . They come into sync; her hormones are bathing him. Her . . . neurochemicals are bathing him or her, and there's this deep affinity at birth.[13]

AN ADOPTEE'S EXPERIENCE

Taryn, twenty-nine, can affirm that losing a biological mother as an infant can profoundly affect a person. Adopted at four months, Taryn is an intelligent Christian woman who is very close to her adoptive parents. She didn't suffer from severe abuse or neglect as an orphan. Nevertheless, Taryn has struggled all her life with the fear of being abandoned by those she loves. She has learned that this unconscious fear stems from the trauma she experienced when she was separated from her birth mother.

Throughout Taryn's childhood, her unconscious fear of rejection would cause her to shut down emotionally. She found it difficult to communicate with those closest to her, but she didn't understand *why* she couldn't seem to respond to her parents. Now that she's an adult, she realizes that she feared being rejected if she gave a "wrong" answer.

"When I was younger, my parents would ask for eye contact," Taryn says. "This was a way to communicate that I was hearing them and listening. Even if it is difficult to find the words, I think eye contact can be a form of respect to those who are patiently wading the emotional waters with you. And there would be times when it was easier for me to write what I was feeling or draw pictures to communicate what I could not say. Also, I appreciated a lot of yes or no questions. My mom was great at guessing, and it made it easier to just nod."

As an adult, Taryn found herself having this same problem with her boyfriend, who is now her husband. Knowing how vital communication is in a marriage, she sought counseling, where she was encouraged to face her abandonment trauma.

"I learned that cognition and emotion are intertwined," she notes, "so even if I knew I wanted to communicate better, I had to deal with the emotions tied to old cognitions—like people will leave me if they don't like what I have to say."

Although Taryn still struggles to express herself with those she loves, especially during times of intense emotion, change, or conflict, she and her husband are working together to increase trust and develop new communication patterns. Her husband realizes that Taryn may only be able to give him short answers initially. Sometimes even short answers are difficult for her to supply, and she needs time to process her thoughts. The couple have also developed a type of shorthand with each other, which defuses conflict.

"My husband needs to know what kind of emotion we are dealing with," explains Taryn. "Am I mad, am I sad, am I working through how I'm feeling, or do I need something? So if I'm in the midst of shutting down [emotionally], I try, because of my love for him, to find the few words to articulate what type of emotion I'm feeling. If I cannot identify it, I try my best to at least say that. He not only greatly appreciates this but also feels respected."

Continued, repeated affirmation that her loved ones won't desert her also helps her grow in this area. "My mom still tells me that my abandonment ended when I became her daughter," she says with a smile.

BE INFORMED

Like Taryn, your new child may also be wounded. That's why it's so important to understand these very real adoption issues. When we know the source of our children's behaviors, it helps us respond in healing ways. Accepting the fact that your new child is likely to have wounds is the first step in seeing beyond certain behaviors and into your child's heart.

Following are a few useful books that can deepen your knowledge about how to parent wounded children:

- *The Connected Child*, by Karyn Purvis and David Cross. Written by two research psychologists specializing in adoption and attachment, this book offers ideas for building bonds of affection and trust with your child. Purvis also wrote *Created to Connect: A Christian's Guide to The Connected Child*, which you can download for free at http://empoweredtoconnect.org/guide. The guide is designed to help illuminate the biblical principles that serve as the foundation for the philosophy and interventions detailed in *The Connected Child*.

- *Adopting the Hurt Child* and *Parenting the Hurt Child*, by Gregory C. Keck and Regina M. Kupecky. These books were lifesavers for me, offering parent-friendly, practical, and hopeful how-to advice from two respected experts on how to help your child heal from emotional wounds.

- *Wounded Children, Healing Homes*, by Jayne E. Schooler, Betsey Keefer Smalley, and Timothy J. Callahan, not only explains how traumatized children impact adoptive and foster families but also offers strategies for successful parenting. One important chapter discusses how the children you already have at home can be adversely affected, and how parents can avoid this risk.

- *Attaching in Adoption: Practical Tools for Today's Parents*, by Deborah D. Gray. This classic book explains what attachment is, how grief and trauma can affect children's emotional development, and how to improve attachment, respect, cooperation, and trust.

- *Handbook on Thriving as an Adoptive Family*, published by Focus on the Family and written by adoptive parents and counselors. This book offers a wide range of information, including chapters on life issues for adoptees from infancy to adolescence.

- *The Body Keeps the Score: Brain, Mind, and Body in the Healing of Trauma*, by Bessel van der Kolk, MD. Published in 2014 and written by a leading researcher in emotional trauma, this book explains the latest science on how the brain works, how it's affected by trauma, and what new treatments are helping. Part three of the book focuses on the minds of children.

If your child comes from a background of abuse and neglect or has experienced the foster-care system or an orphanage, it's important to be aware of what's called *complex trauma*. As opposed to acute trauma caused by a single event, complex trauma is "the experience of multiple, chronic, and prolonged, developmentally adverse traumatic events, most often of an interpersonal nature."[14]

A child who experiences this type of trauma needs parents who are willing to learn nontraditional child-rearing principles called *trauma-informed parenting*. Organizations like the Karen Purvis Institute of Child Development (child.tcu.edu) offer research-based strategies and teaching DVDs so parents can be equipped to help children heal.

Our new son had been deeply wounded during his first twelve years of life, but we didn't know all the details at first. The information came out in bits and pieces as we went to therapy and talked at home.

At age three, Daniel found his father hanging by a noose, an image so haunting that I had to ask a teacher not to play the hangman word game while my son was in class. Daniel's mother was an alcoholic who often left her children alone, and when Daniel was just seven, the police showed up one day along with a van from the orphanage. That was last time he saw his mother.

Because Daniel was malnourished, he was sent to a hospital and then later to an orphanage a great distance from his home. He and his sister never saw their grandparents and older half siblings again, and Daniel lost the only photo they had of their mother—a fact that not only grieved him but also made him condemn himself, even though he was only a little boy at the time.

The orphanage was a brutal place. Because the night woman in charge said Daniel talked too much, he was forced to kneel with bare knees on salt poured over the hard wooden floors. The morning after, he could barely walk. The bigger boys also beat him regularly.

I didn't know what to call it at the time, but now I would say our son experienced complex trauma. When we arrived at the orphanage in Russia, we discovered that Daniel had jumped off a roof, pretending to be Spider-Man and injuring his leg. Exterior wounds heal easily, but the inner wounds—the ones more difficult to see, understand, and heal—require the most of a parent.

Because of that fact, it's *extremely* important to seek professional help if your child has a complex past. Seek all the resources available to you as you love your new child. Of course, faith is the firm foundation we all need as we face the reality of wounded children.

"You may encounter unplanned and unexpected obstacles in your journey," says Debi Grebenik, executive director of a foster-care program in Colorado and a licensed clinical social worker. "Faith is staying power when love wanes. It enables you to see your children's needs from God's perspective."[15]

Carrie Blaske knows firsthand about the sustaining power of faith in God and what that can mean when you are nursing wounded children. She and her husband adopted several children in 2008, and they know that kids who have been hurt in the past often react as if they are facing danger. Something in their environment may trigger a memory of abuse or neglect. A slamming door, a certain word, or even a smell can instantly send them into a state of fear and panic. These are called triggers, and they are unique to each child. When a child is triggered, the amygdala—the part of the brain most connected to anger and fear—becomes fully engaged, and no amount of reasoning will calm a child in that moment.

For Carrie and her family, dealing with such triggers often means not actually being together as a family when they've planned to be. Here's how she explains it:

> Oftentimes, we go out to eat but end up with some of us eating, and two of us in another part of the restaurant "working down" from a trigger. Once when I was in the other part of the restaurant with one kiddo but still had a view of the rest of my family eating, I found myself fighting all kinds of emotions. I still needed to be present, stay calm, address the need, stick close to confront behavior—all while hearing my stomach churn with hunger and my heart beating about as fast as my thoughts were swirling. While sticking close to this kiddo, I kept hearing, *If this were you having the trigger, how would you like to be treated?*

Carrie managed to help calm her child; then the rest of the family drove home in her oldest son's car while Carrie loaded her boxed food and the struggling child into her vehicle. She recalls,

> On the drive home, I was thinking through the situation, recounting how we roll through similar situations every week. Then I felt my heart shift as the Holy Spirit gave me a picture of the Shepherd leaving the ninety-nine to go after the one [Luke 15:4-6]. I honestly can't count how many times my husband and I are leaving—excusing ourselves from a

family activity—to go get the *one*. Even if the *one* isn't physically away, that child needs to be pursued, known, seen, heard, and brought back into the group.

As I sat in the car, I pondered being triggered and how I would want those who say they love me most to treat me. I pondered the time the Lord left the ninety-nine for me—the one lost and hurting. On that day—for the measure I personally needed so I could be present for this kiddo—I was met and cared for by the Lord. Even when "being with the family" often doesn't equal being together, I'm still good!

THE REALITY OF JOY

As you consider the reality of wounded children, know that the joy of being a parent is just as real. Along with the typical joys of being a parent, there can also be a deeper joy that comes from overcoming difficulties and seeing your child heal.

Several years ago a couple adopted a medically fragile girl as well as an infant boy with congestive heart failure. "The first five months were just keeping him alive," the mother says. "We didn't think he would be talking before age five because his delays were immense. But now he's four, and his vocabulary and comprehension are absolutely remarkable. . . . There are still challenges and struggles, but we have active, joyful, amazing children who have taught us so much about life and overcoming hard things."

Healing from emotional wounds can also bring joy. It's no wonder a young boy from the foster-care system had nightmares for a year after being adopted and always needed the bedroom light on; he had been abused so badly, he almost died. The joy came when the nightmares finally ended, his adoptive father remembers. This man was able to tuck his son into bed and hear him say, "Dad, you can turn the light off. I don't need it anymore."

Another adoptive mom describes the joy of adopting an older boy. "Our first year together had many struggles," she observes. "It was the hardest year of my life, but it's been the most rewarding, too."

Whatever earthly reality you may face in adoption or as a parent, you can fully rely on this: God's love won't disappear (Isaiah 41:10; Romans 8:38-39), God knows you (1 Corinthians 8:3), and God wants to have a relationship with you (Revelation 3:20).

Diana Stone lost three sons shortly after giving birth to them, and she also suffered through failed adoptions. Yet she reached this conclusion: "My prayers and my life are for the glory of God, no matter the circumstances or the outcome. This isn't about me; it's all about him. And in my heart and soul, I know that he makes everything beautiful in its time."[16]

Rest Stop

1. As you consider the unknowns of adoption and the realities involved, don't forget these "knowns" of God:
   - God knows the distress of your soul (Psalm 31:7).
   - He knows the exact number of days you will live (Psalm 139:16) and the number of hairs on your head (Luke 12:7).
   - He reveals "hidden things" we cannot know without Him (Isaiah 48:6; Jeremiah 33:3).
   - Those who love God are "known by God" (1 Corinthians 8:3).
   - Jesus came to make God known (John 1:18).

2. Ask God to make Himself known to you.

3. Record your thoughts about the realities of adoption on the journal page.

My Journey to Adoption

DATE _____

The LORD watches over the foreigner and
sustains the fatherless and the widow.

Psalm 146:9, NIV

CHAPTER 4

Facing Fear

When the cares of my heart are many,
your consolations cheer my soul.

PSALM 94:19

Once you've examined your expectations and considered the realities of adoption, you might be apprehensive about the unknown. You wouldn't be the first parent to feel anxious at various points throughout the adoption process and after bringing your child home.

If you're feeling this way, hang tightly to what Jeremiah 6:16 tells us: "Ask for the ancient paths, where the good way is; and walk in it, and find rest for your souls." Bring your fears to the One who can replace them with peace and direction.

At one point, fear almost stopped me from obeying what God had called us to do. Because Jeff and I had to attend forty hours of classes to become licensed as foster parents, my eyes were opened to the multitude of ways a child can be hurt—emotionally and physically—and how those wounds could manifest themselves in unpleasant and difficult ways. As Jeff and I read—with pain—the profiles of various foster children over several months, we learned through graphic descriptions about some of the abuse, indignities, neglect, and lack of stability these kids had faced.

Were we ready to parent a child diagnosed with fetal alcohol spectrum disorder (FASD) or reactive attachment disorder (RAD)? The thought terrified me.

Children available for adoption may have developmental delays, post-traumatic stress disorder (PTSD), attention deficit hyperactivity disorder (ADHD), oppositional defiant disorder (ODD), and/or attachment disorders. They may behave in ways that have become automatic survival skills for them: lying, stealing, hoarding food, manipulating, or treating the mother differently than the father and pitting them against each other.

FASD

If a woman drinks alcohol during pregnancy, her child is at risk for developing a fetal alcohol spectrum disorder (FASD). This term covers a range of disabilities.

- Children in foster care are ten to fifteen times more likely to be affected by prenatal alcohol exposure than other children.[1]
- A birth family history of mental illness or drug or alcohol abuse increases the risk of a child's having FASD. Sadly, three-quarters of the children in foster care have that type of family history.[2]

ATTACHMENT DISORDERS

When children in their earliest years try to bond with their primary caregivers but discover that it only ends in pain, hurt, neglect, or traumatic disruptions, they learn to protect themselves and not trust adults. They learn to push people away and control their environment. Attachment disorder is treatable, but parents should seek highly qualified attachment therapists to receive a proper diagnosis and assistance.

This dysfunction in a child's ability to trust and to give and receive love can be mild in some children and extremely severe in others. Severe attachment issues are diagnosed as reactive attachment disorder (RAD).

According to the Institute for Attachment and Child Development in Littleton, Colorado, children with RAD are greatly affected by fear stemming from the pain of their first few years of life, so they try to control their main caregiver (usually the adoptive mother) to protect themselves:

> The brains of children with RAD look different from the brains of children who didn't experience trauma. Reactive attachment disorder is a brain injury that typically occurs as a result of early abuse and neglect. . . .
>
> When people experience traumatic events, the stress hormone cortisol gets released in the brain. This biochemical reaction to chronic and extreme stress changes the formation of the brain.[3]

If children experience trauma before the age of five, their brains can be "stuck" developmentally at early ages. "Their behaviors can look similar to that of a younger child. They steal, lie, argue, throw temper tantrums, blame others for their mistakes, and have trouble regulating their emotions."[4] (For stories about children who were diagnosed with RAD and received successful treatment, see www.attachment.org/can-children-heal-from-rad/.)

Every foster-care class Jeff and I attended seemed to present an additional disorder that we might encounter. I was more than a little frightened, and God knew it.

SLAYING THE GIANTS

My group Bible study at that time just happened to focus on the Israelites crossing the wilderness after being freed from slavery in Egypt. After God's people had made a short trek through the desert, God was ready to bring them into the Promised Land. Unfortunately, most of the Israelite spies were paralyzed with fear after they saw the people they would have to battle in Canaan. Here's what they reported:

> The people who dwell in the land are strong, and the cities are fortified and very large. And besides, we saw the descendants of Anak there. (Numbers 13:28)

> We are not able to go up against the people, for they are stronger than we are. (verse 31)

> All the people that we saw in [the land] are of great height. . . . We seemed to ourselves like grasshoppers, and so we seemed to them. (verses 32-33)

As I read these verses, it was clear to me that I could have been one of those fainthearted spies, even though I was a woman born in the twentieth century. I was a grasshopper, and FASD, RAD, and the rest of the alphabet soup of disorders were the giants. But God wasn't finished talking with me. He reminded me of Caleb, an Israelite who saw the giants but had a different attitude:

> Caleb quieted the people before Moses and said, "Let us go up at once and occupy [the land], for we are well able to overcome it." (verse 30)

> Do not fear the people of the land. . . . The LORD is with us; do not fear them. (Numbers 14:9)

God was clearly looking for this type of trust and obedience from His children, since He told the Israelites,

> Not one of [the men] who saw my glory and the signs I performed in Egypt and in the wilderness but who

disobeyed me and tested me ten times—not one of them will ever see the land I promised on oath to their ancestors. No one who has treated me with contempt will ever see it. But because my servant Caleb has a different spirit and *follows me wholeheartedly*, I will bring him into the land he went to, and his descendants will inherit it. (Numbers 14:22-24, NIV; emphasis added)

I heard God speaking to my quaking spirit through this Old Testament story: *I know adoption is scary. Adopting is like facing the giants in the Promised Land. But trust Me; I can handle the giants. I need you to follow Me wholeheartedly, like Caleb did.*

The Lord's reassurance helped me move forward in obedience with my husband. A child's wounds can be serious; they can look as menacing as a ten-foot-tall warrior. The only way to conquer fear of the unknown is by following those ancient paths, the paths that lead to the Lord.

GOD IS EVERYWHERE

Fear can strike in many ways before you actually bring a child into your home. Bruce and Sue Kaul faced their "giant" as they traveled overseas to meet the children they were planning to adopt. This couple never aspired to be world travelers, but on April 4, 2005, they found themselves on a wild ride to Stavropol, Russia, a city near the border of Chechnya, the republic that had been fighting with Russia for independence.

The Kauls went even though the US State Department had included this part of Russia on its Travel Warnings list, and despite Sue's desire to stay close to her rural Wisconsin home and Bruce's habit of becoming nervous on plane rides. They boarded a plane because they were convinced that God wanted them to adopt two young Russian boys. The first step in the process was meeting the boys at an orphanage.

After the Kauls landed in Moscow, a guide drove them to a smaller airport where they would catch a plane to Stavropol. From the start, the trip was stressful. First, they climbed onto the wrong shuttle at the airport.

"Stavropol?" Bruce asked a Russian man.

"Nyet!"

Pushing their way out of the jammed bus, Bruce and Sue heard annoyed natives mumbling, *"Amerikanski!"*

"We felt lost and vulnerable, not to mention hungry and tired after thirty hours of traveling and no sleep," Sue recalls.

And finally seeing the tiny Russian plane they were about to board did nothing to ease their growing fears. They stood on the tarmac staring at the dilapidated aircraft as its engines fired. Both of them felt sick from the mist of burning fuel. On the way to her seat, Sue tripped on a ripped piece of carpet and peered at the metal body of the plane through holes in the floor covering. Stuffing erupted from the seat cushions. That's when she started to worry. Would they make it to Stavropol?

After the plane landed at 11:00 p.m., the pilot made an announcement in Russian that Bruce and Sue couldn't understand. The Russian passengers groaned in response, so the couple knew something bad had happened, but what? They sat in their seats for forty-five minutes on a pitch-black runway. *Where are the airport building's lights?* they wondered. Finally the passengers were allowed off the plane.

"We were shocked to see military men carrying machine guns," Sue says. "They had lined up, creating a corridor for us to walk through. I was terrified."

The only light this exhausted midwestern couple saw came from the headlights of military trucks, fire engines, and ambulances. There they were, in the dark of night facing machine guns in a foreign country with thousands of dollars (adoption payments) strapped to their bodies. They weren't allowed to collect their luggage, so they stood in a parking lot until all the Russian business travelers had driven away.

They were supposed to meet a man named Alex, but where was he? After what seemed like an eternity to the anxious couple, a man tapped Bruce on the shoulder. Alex couldn't speak much English, but the Kauls later learned that Chechen fighters had threatened to bomb the airport, which explained why it was blacked out and soldiers had surrounded the plane.

When Alex left the couple at their hotel room on the thirteenth floor, he pointed to his watch. "Six," he said in a heavy Russian accent. "We see boys."

The trauma of the travel and the night was too much for Sue. When she remembered that they would have to travel twice to Russia before they could bring the children home, she fell apart, crying on the hotel bed. She wondered how she could make this trip again. Not only that, but she had doubts about the adoption. They hadn't even seen the boys yet.

"I felt so out of control and helpless," she recalls.

Bruce began to pray, expressing the couple's fears, thanking God for bringing them to Stavropol safely, and asking for renewed faith and peace. Sue finally fell asleep to her husband's voice. Two hours later, the alarm rang. It was 6:00 a.m.

"Are you ready to meet your kids?" Bruce asked his wife as he stood by the window.

"I don't know," she said.

FEAR NOT

Sue was still in bed when Bruce opened the curtains to a sight she would never forget. From where she was lying, she stared at a marble angel perfectly framed by the window.

"It looked like a painting hanging in the sky, especially for me," she says. Against the backdrop of a predawn sky, the angel statue rested on a high column, its wings outspread, its arms lifting a cross to the sky.

You're supposed to be here, God whispered to Sue at that moment. *You're going to be fine. Get out of bed and do what I want you to do.*

A feeling of God's protection settled on Sue as she looked at that angel. She sensed God saying to her, *Even though you are far away from everything familiar, Sue, I'm still here. Even though nothing around you seems dependable, I'm still with you.*

It's common to see memorials and statues in Russia paying homage to World War II heroes or Communist-era leaders like Lenin, but an angel carrying a cross is an unexpected sight. The Kauls knew God had placed them in that specific hotel room to reassure them.

The airport incident wasn't the end of their trials in Russia, but nothing overwhelmed the couple after seeing that angel. Even discovering that the boys had a fourteen-year-old sister didn't cause Sue and Bruce to doubt God's plan. And when they faced a decision about adopting the girl, their faith didn't waver even though they didn't have the eight thousand dollar fee.

"We knew God would take care of it," Sue says. (And He did.)

On that morning in the hotel room, God had given them the peace and renewed faith Bruce had prayed for.

"When my world fell apart in that Russian hotel room, it forced me to give complete control to God," Sue reflects. "When times are tough and I forget God is in control, I remember that angel."

Fear may strike you at some point during your adoption journey, but if you turn to God as the Kauls did, He will fill you with boldness and faith.

WHAT DO YOU SEE?

As Christina Bothel and her husband try to help their children heal from early wounds, they've felt anxious at times. But one day God not only calmed their fears; He also gave them a new perspective. Using the familiar story of David and Goliath in 1 Samuel 17, God shared with the Bothels the reason for the young shepherd boy's victory:

> God showed us that when David walked onto that battlefield, he didn't see the size of the giant, the size of his weapons, the size of the enemy army, or the battlefield itself. David saw his God and how big He is. His eyes were fixed on God. David moved forward on that battlefield with confidence because he knew who his confidence was in.

Now when the Bothels momentarily lose their focus, they sense God asking them, *Are you looking at the giant? The size of the army? The battlefield?*

"When we focus on the giants, the battlefield, or the enemy army, we let fear and anxiety creep in," Christina says. "Suddenly we feel like fools. We think, *What are we doing on this battlefield anyway? This is impossible!* It's only when our eyes are fixed on how big our God is that we see hope where we shouldn't see hope, we have peace when we shouldn't have peace, and our giants become translucent. With spiritual eyes, we see fighting alongside us an army of warriors with the same foolish confidence. The landscape changes."

How about you? What do you see? Are you looking at giant fears or a powerful, loving God who is on your side? Remember, it was God who protected the Israelites and destroyed the Amorites, "whose height was like the height of the cedars and who [were] as strong as the oaks" (Amos 2:9). God can also handle your fears.

 ## Rest Stop

What giants of fear are you facing? List them on the journal page. Then write a prayer to God, asking Him to slay those fears.

My Journey to Adoption

DATE _____

Fear not, for I am with you; be not dismayed, for
I am your God; I will strengthen you, I will help you,
I will uphold you with my righteous right hand.

Isaiah 41:10

CHAPTER 5

Listening to God

*This thing I did command them: "Listen to and obey My voice,
and I will be your God, and you shall be My people; and you will walk
in all the way which I command you, so that it may be well with you."*

JEREMIAH 7:23, AMP

As I began to think and pray about the possibility of adoption, I sensed God replying to every doubt and question in my mind. But Jeff wasn't convinced that adoption was God's plan for us.

"Maybe God is asking us to take care of orphans without adopting one," he said. "There are other ways to support orphans."

True, but the next day I heard a specific answer from God as I pulled the Times Square Church newsletter out of my mailbox. In it was an impassioned message by the late Pastor David Wilkerson about how the Lord had shown him he must become personally involved in caring for widows and orphans.

My dialogue with God continued, but I sensed resistance from Jeff. Then one Sunday morning, I asked God to speak to us at church if He really wanted us to adopt. Maybe if Jeff and I heard God's call at the same time, we could settle this question.

As I sat in the pew next to Jeff, our pastor—who knew nothing of our thoughts of adoption—started his sermon with these words: "Today I'm going to talk about my favorite subject: adoption!"

When the pastor said he was adopted, the entire congregation gasped. No one knew. After a pause, he clarified: "We're all adopted, adopted by God as children of God." He was no stranger to this topic, however; he and his wife had adopted three infants.

God wanted to make sure we heard His message that day, because at the end of the sermon, our pastor said this: "I urge anyone to adopt a child, even if you already have children."

I was sure that sealed the deal, but when I asked Jeff if he had heard God speaking to him, he simply said no.

I was confused, and I let God know it. *Lord, Jeff says he doesn't hear You, and You know I can't obey You on this unless he clearly knows this is Your will for us.*

From then on, I concentrated on praying that Jeff would clearly hear what the Lord had to say to him—whatever that was. I had to keep my mouth shut and pray. I decided that if my husband didn't hear from God as I had, there would be no adoption.

The decision to adopt can happen in many different ways. One of you might be convinced that adoption is precisely what God wants you to do, while the other might be dead set against it. Or both of you might be sure right away and then begin to doubt when the finances don't come through or obstacles make the process difficult.

In our case, Jeff eventually agreed that God was calling us

to adopt. Once he was sure, there was no turning back. At least that's what I thought.

THE SWITCH

Here's what I discovered: Sometimes adoption can be a long process, longer than the nine months it takes to give birth to an infant. (But not always! I recently spoke with a couple who welcomed all three of their adopted children into their home within one week of learning about them.)

As the process of adoption drags on, God often works in our hearts, changing us and growing us spiritually. Even if you had a billboard from God telling you to adopt a child, doubts could still creep into your mind later on, and you would need to continue listening for God's direction throughout the process.

At the time Jeff and I began the adoption process, I'd been a parent for twelve years—and a good one, I thought. But after attending forty hours of foster-care classes and learning about the behaviors a traumatized child could bring into our home, I balked.

As the classes revealed the survival techniques that children develop to cope with their fractured world, I found a new appreciation for our family. The typical concerns of arguing teens, chores left undone, or an occasional bad grade were nothing compared to what these children in the foster-care system were dealing with.

Our family of four enjoyed each other's company and shared similar interests. There were no major struggles or conflicts in our home. Our life together was peaceful and fun. I suddenly realized that once we adopted a child, our happy nuclear family would never be the same again. I began to grieve the family we were at that point in time. Our family as I knew it would be gone forever. That made me sad. And I didn't feel adequate for the task of raising a wounded child.

One night I couldn't sleep. As I lay awake in the middle of the night, trying to remember a certain psalm, God whispered Psalm 82 to my heart. I climbed out of bed and read His message to me: "Give justice to the weak and the fatherless. . . . Rescue the weak and the needy; deliver them from the hand of the wicked" (verses 3-4).

But I still faltered and lingered in my selfishness. I was right back where I started, even after being thoroughly convinced that the Lord had planned for adoption to be part of our lives.

I love my family, I thought. *I don't want it to change. Do we really need to do this?*

God heard the question in my mind, and once again He answered me during a church service. As I listened to a sermon one Sunday, these verses rang in my ears:

> Whoever loves father or mother more than me is not
> worthy of me, and whoever loves son or daughter more
> than me is not worthy of me. And whoever does not
> take his cross and follow me is not worthy of me. . . .
> Whoever loses his life for my sake will find it.
>
> MATTHEW 10:37-39

I obeyed My Father, Jesus said to me through this verse. *I love Him, but I had to leave Him for a while. I sweated blood. I had to give up My life. Now I ask you to do the same. Love Me more than your happy family.*

How could I possibly say no to the Lord?

Jesus also comforted me with these words: "You will grieve, but your grief will turn to joy. A woman giving birth to a child has pain because her time has come; but when her baby is born she forgets the anguish because of her joy that a child is born into the world" (John 16:20-21, NIV).

I'd given birth twice, so I knew that to be true. In fact, as I struggled through painful contractions with my second child, Ben, I screamed to a nurse, "Give me a C-section!"

"Oh, honey," she said, "it's too late for that."

Once the pain was over, those contractions became completely irrelevant when a tsunami of love and deep joy totally obliterated them as I held my beautiful son.

As Jeff and I connected with our new children through adoption, God was gracious to give us that same kind of joy—the joy of receiving new children to love into our lives.

God speaks to people in many different ways as they consider adoption. For Domingo Garcia, His voice was loud and clear on the subject.

A BAT TO THE HEAD

Irene Garcia was passionate about adopting a little girl, but the foster-care social worker told her and her husband, Domingo, that this six-week-old baby might have brain damage. A possible mental disability didn't concern Irene, but Domingo had made it clear that they and their two boys would sacrifice too much if they adopted a child with a severe disorder.

As the couple ordered lunch before the social worker arrived with the baby—she wanted them to at least see the little girl— Domingo figured the adoption would go nowhere. He had played along with his wife's request, betting on his pre-Christian drinking-and-driving record to stop the process. After all, who would approve someone with his past as an adoptive father? That would be his way out of this deal, a way to enjoy his two boys and sacrifice nothing.

As Domingo prayed over their meal that day in 1981, he said it felt as if God "hit [him] with a bat."

"Oh, Irene," he told his wife, "I see it now. Here I am profess-ing to love God, but I'm saying no to Him. That I don't want to take this innocent child. . . . She didn't ask to be born. She's an innocent victim. And I'm so selfish that I don't want to take her because it's inconvenient for me and my family. God is giving me a child. A beautiful gift. Who am I to say no?"[1]

Irene and Domingo went on to adopt many children from the foster-care system. As the baby girl—their daughter Esther—grew older, she became a good caregiver for her younger siblings. Now an adult, she still lives with her parents and plays an impor-tant role in caring for other children from the foster-care system who come into the Garcias' home.

ROUND TWO

Bill and Kim were both forty-two in 2007 when they began listening to God's message about adoption. It began when another couple told them they were adopting children.

I'm in so much trouble, Bill thought that day. He knew his wife had long been interested in adoption and still was, even though two of their biological children were in junior and senior high school and the third was a college student.

Bill agreed to attend an informational meeting on the topic of adoption, but afterward, Kim decided the idea was "dumb" for people their age.

"My heart was there," she recalls, "but my head was saying, *Kim, don't be so silly. Your kids are grown.*"

Even though Bill and Kim didn't pursue adoption, adoption pursued them. The topic "seemed to turn up everywhere" during the next year, Kim says. "We would laugh about it because it was getting ridiculous."

One Sunday in 2008, their pastor mentioned a conference called Wait No More. The event, produced by Focus on the

Family, encouraged people to explore adoption from the foster-care system. They knew they had to attend, Kim says, because they couldn't ignore God's direction any longer.

At the conference, God gave the couple a deep sense of peace. "It wasn't a question anymore," Kim reflects. "It felt like this [was] what obedience is."

Not long after the conference, God hit the fast-forward button, giving this older couple four children who were brothers under the age of seven—all within three days, even though Bill and Kim weren't yet licensed as foster parents.[2]

A LIFE THAT MATTERS

Robbie and Karly Leib listened to God's voice via podcast. To be exact, they heard from Him through a series of sermons by Francis Chan titled "Living a Life That Matters." Because this series deeply affected Robbie, he kept suggesting that Karly also listen to the podcasts.

One day Karly finally played a sermon titled "Is Suffering Optional?" By reading verses from every book of the Bible, Chan pointed out that Christians are called to suffer for the gospel.

One verse in particular stood out to the Leibs: "It has been granted to you that for the sake of Christ you should not only believe in him but also suffer for his sake" (Philippians 1:29).

Karly understood that Chan was calling Christians to change their perspective from "How can I avoid suffering?" to "How can I glorify God and spread the gospel, regardless of the sacrifice?" Then Chan posed this question to his listeners: "Is there anything we can do to look more like Christ than to rescue people?" Life, he said, should be about sacrifice and rescue, because that's what Jesus' life was about.

"God used these words to do a work in my heart that day," Karly reflects. "And He called me into a deeper relationship with

Him built on faith, sacrifice, and obedience. Robbie and I were both convicted that we had been setting up our lives in such a way as to intentionally avoid suffering. Over the next few weeks, I prayed daily about what this meant in my life, and I asked God how I could surrender my life for Him."

It was at that point in 2009 that the couple felt the Lord calling them to the ministry of foster adoption. Nine months later, the Leibs were licensed foster parents.

But just days after they received their license, the couple learned some devastating news. Their close friends' healthy four-month-old son, Zeke, had died of SIDS (sudden infant death syndrome). The Leibs and their three children were left reeling from the loss, and they grieved deeply with their dearest friends.

The couple didn't expect that Zeke's death would profoundly affect their view of foster care as a ministry, but it did.

"It became clear to us that God is the one who decides how long each of our children will be in our home, whether we give birth to them, foster them, or adopt them," Karly says. "As crazy as it sounds, Zeke's death actually brought us into a deeper place of surrender to God. We chose to entrust all of our children to God and count each day with them as an undeserved gift."

Less than two weeks later, a social worker asked Robbie and Karly to take in a baby boy who had been born that very day.

"We both knew we were supposed to say yes," Karly recalls. (Read more about the Leibs' story in chapter 8.)

IS IT GOD?

God can use anything to gain our attention, but we must make the choice to listen to Him and obey. Perhaps you haven't heard God's voice before, or you're unsure that what you heard was from Him. This was true for my friend Sue, who with her husband, Dave, had quickly and easily brought home a Chinese baby girl while they lived and worked in China. But securing official adoption papers was a more difficult task.

Years went by—three to be exact—as they exhausted all means of receiving the papers. They wouldn't be able to take their daughter out of the country without government approval of the adoption.

"We had contacted everyone who knew anyone who was connected to someone who might have influence to get things rolling again," Sue recalls. And then God's words to Moses caught her eye: "Stand still, and see the salvation of the LORD" (Exodus 14:13, NKJV).

"I had the distinct impression that we were to cease striving, to stop doing anything except wait. But I didn't know for sure if God really spoke that way. It was new to me. But we followed that prompting, and soon the official called and told us to come sign the papers!"

As you listen for God's voice, remember that His message to you will always align with His Word. Sue found one classic book on this topic helpful: *Hearing God: Developing a Conversational Relationship with God* by Dallas Willard.

If you are still unsure if God is calling you to adopt, continue to ask Him for direction and for sensitivity to His message. If you and your spouse don't agree about adoption, pray that God would make His voice clear to both of you so you will be unified.

Rest Stop

Are you listening to God's voice? What have you heard? Record it on your journal page, along with any questions you have for the Lord.

My Journey to Adoption

DATE _____

Whoever is of God hears the words of God.

John 8:47

PART 2

During the Process

CHAPTER 6

Gathering Support

The gospel is not a picture of adoption;
adoption is a picture of the gospel.

JOHN PIPER
pastor and author

Welcoming a child into your home and your life is definitely something to celebrate. Yet an adoption is often just the beginning of a child's healing process. Chances are you'll be helping this child heal from loss, trauma, or developmental delays, and that isn't a simple thing to do. Yes, the process can be rewarding and beautiful, but it can also be exhausting, frightening, confusing, and extremely frustrating.

Picture this: Your child is playing in the living room and suddenly starts screaming. And you have no idea why. It takes time for you to realize that the man on the TV with that loud voice reminds your daughter of her abuser.

I never did figure out why Daniel reacted in panic and fear to some things. Why, for instance, did he start panicking that day as Jeff and I watched a videotape of our wedding?

Challenges such as these are why you will need other people by your side. Building a support network as soon as you can is preventive medicine that will go a long way toward safeguarding your marriage, your family, and your new child's future.

During our first difficult year with Daniel, we had to deal with his post-traumatic stress disorder, severe anxiety, lack of trust, explosive anger, defiance, and desire to run away as well as punish himself.

At first we didn't understand where his behaviors were coming from and what they meant, let alone know how to respond to them in a healthy way. Our therapist once said to me, "It's like you're running a residential treatment center." Except we weren't trained therapists, and we were on duty 24/7! Looking back, I see we needed more support than we had.

In a *Focus on the Family* interview, author Tricia Goyer recalled her initial belief that parenting adopted children from the foster-care system would be no different from the way she and her husband, John, had raised their biological kids.

"[Our new children] came in with so many issues, I was completely overwhelmed. But [we turned] to friends who also adopted from foster care, [and] we got them into some great therapy that really helped," Tricia said. "It was a lot harder than I originally thought, but also a bigger blessing than I originally thought."[1]

WHY SUPPORT IS NEEDED

There are several other reasons for gathering a support system:

1. *You'll need a listening, empathetic ear.* Friends raising children who aren't affected by loss, trauma, or special needs and people who aren't educated about adoption won't understand how you parent your new child or the

significance of your struggles and victories. Unless you connect with other parents who understand your life, this can lead to feelings of isolation and may even cause you to doubt your ability to parent. Likewise, some family members may simply tune you out, saying your child's behaviors are "just a phase." Find a few listening and understanding ears now.

2. *Satan doesn't like orphans or adoptive parents.* He hates to see the gospel displayed for all the world to see, and adoption is the perfect representation of our Father's unconditional love. Satan wants to keep that child you adopted far from God, so put on your spiritual armor (Ephesians 6:13) and recruit others to pray with you. (See chapters 13 and 14 about spiritual battles.)

3. *Welcoming a new child into your life takes time and energy.* You'll need someone to give you a break so you can regain your physical, mental, and emotional strength. When children have been hurt or are processing loss, they can act strangely, so you'll need extra stamina to be a behavioral detective.

You might have to ask yourself, "What is this child communicating to me when he bangs his head into the wall or turns into a statue and won't respond to me?"

"Why is she so sad on her birthday?"

"Why does our toddler have a screaming fit each time Mom enters the bathroom and shuts the door?"

For one couple, the answer to the last question was this: Their two-year-old knew that when his birth mom entered the bathroom, she did drugs and wouldn't come out for a day. Then he would be in his dirty diaper and all alone for a long time. He expected the same thing to happen with his new mother, so he protested each time his adoptive mom shut the bathroom door.

MANDATORY SUPPORT

In Denver, Colorado, a Christian adoption ministry called Project 1.27 (based on James 1:27) *requires* prospective adoptive parents to recruit four support people. President Shelly Radic, who is also an adoptive mother, says that during the first years with her new children, she was afraid to share their family's struggles with anyone because she feared being judged. But when her family moved to Colorado, she worked hard to develop a support system.

One night, after a difficult day with the children, Shelly says she was too weary and discouraged to pray. That's when she received this text from her adoptive moms prayer group: "For those of you who are too weary to pray anymore, I will take the night watch. Sleep soundly."

"And I did sleep soundly that night," Shelly says.

"We've had families at Project 1.27 who at first think the idea of a support network is dumb, and they're resistant. But later they are so thankful they have it," Shelly adds. Because Project 1.27 spends four hours providing basic information to support team members, these people are equipped with foundational knowledge of adoption issues.

THANKFUL FAMILIES

Parenting three siblings ages one, two, and five after adopting them from the foster-care system was even more exhausting than Jeff and Jessamy Johnson had imagined.[2] Going instantly from zero children to three toddlers isn't normal to begin with, and these kids presented "challenging behaviors" that included "lengthy, violent fits full of screaming and spitting."

In addition to that, the couple spent an inordinate amount of time transporting the children to multiple weekly medical and therapy appointments. The kids were "sick all the time" because they hadn't received proper nutrition in their young lives. That combination was a recipe for exhaustion and stress!

"Parenting is hard enough without the heartache of parenting kids you don't know, who are broken by circumstances you can't understand," Jessamy observes.

But the Johnsons weren't alone in their struggle. A group of friends, family, and church volunteers provided long-term support to the family.

"We had a date night pretty much every week for three years because of their commitment," Jessamy says. "That saved our marriage and made this possible."

Three years later, those once-neglected kids were completely different. The healing the couple has seen in the children is "a total testimony to God's grace, the power of family, and people committed to help," she adds.

Adam and Janai Kane of Albuquerque, New Mexico, were in the process of adopting two boys when they were surprised by a new development: Janai unexpectedly became pregnant.[3] But that wasn't the end of the surprises. Ten days before Janai gave birth, they learned the boys had a newborn sibling. That child, Micah, had been exposed to methamphetamines and had special needs. They wanted to adopt him, too.

"I don't think we could have taken on Micah and made it through without the support of our community," Adam says.

One family cared for Micah for a month. Gifts of meals, clothing, cribs, child care, and laundry services were vital to the health of their home. Members of their church also supported them spiritually with prayer, asking the couple each week for specific requests.

"We've known people who've gone through this [adoption]

with fewer major transitions than we've had, and they've had a lot harder time," Adam points out. "I attribute that to the fact that either they didn't have a church community that came around them, or they weren't as open to the help. It takes both sides."

BEGIN BY ASKING

So how can you recruit people to support you?

First, ask God to provide a support team. Then take action. Don't be too proud to ask. If you have a few trusted friends or relatives who live nearby, invite them to your home and let them know how adopting a child might affect your life in the near future.

Educate them about adoption and how a child may be hurt because of his or her past. Tell them that raising a child who has been neglected or abused requires different parenting strategies. Share some examples from this book. Then take a deep breath and ask them for help.

Help can come in many different forms. Babysitting, prayer support, rides to therapy appointments, grocery shopping, meals, changing the oil in the car, and respite care are just a few examples.

Next, see if there are any adoptive-parent support groups in your church or area. If there are, start attending meetings or events. If there aren't, ask people if they know other adoptive parents in your church, and then introduce yourself to them.

You could also attend a conference for adoptive parents and connect to the social-media groups some offer. (For a list of conferences, see the appendix.) Building a community of like-minded parents is important. God didn't intend for us to be solo Christians; He meant for us to be part of a body.

By the way, are you part of the body of Christ? Do you have a church family to support you as you welcome a new child into your life?

When we adopted Daniel and Masha, our church family threw a shower for us, even though our new kids were ten and eleven. They provided needed items, including sheets, dishes, backpacks, and clothing. Several people prayed faithfully for our new children, and one woman created a special scrapbook for us that has become a precious reminder of how Daniel and Masha joined our family.

If you have biological children, don't forget that they may also need support as they adjust to a new sibling. Are there friends or relatives who can give them a break from the changes at home if you cannot? Will your children be able to continue taking part in the activities they are participating in now? How will their lives change? Can you arrange for a babysitter so you can spend time alone with your biological children? Can you connect your kids to any peers who would understand their situation? Let them know that their needs are just as important as the new child's.

If you have trouble gathering support, remember that nothing is impossible with God (Luke 1:37). We had no idea we would need people who understood our circumstances, but God did. He made sure we met a couple new to our church who was also considering adoption. In fact, they were already signed up for the foster-care classes we were about to begin in a town thirty miles away.

This was no small thing in our tiny town. We were able to journey together with this couple through the process, as well as the joys and difficulties that came later. They were the only other people who truly understood what was happening in our home. God provided what we didn't even know we needed.

God recently made sure another couple began the adoption process with support and education. Even though Jodi and Austin decided to attend an adoption conference at the last minute, God supplied all they needed so they could get there—people who changed their work schedule for Austin, money for the cost of the conference, friends they could stay with while at the conference, and grandparents who would babysit their other children.

CAMPING WITH GOD

God also provided a community of support for Sara and Aaron just when they needed it most. The couple adopted three children, each with special needs. They experienced the benefit of community when they attended the Refresh Conference for adoptive parents, which takes place each February in a suburb of Seattle, Washington. Sara arranged for respite care so they could attend.

"We had literally seven people to cover the three days, including my mother-in-law, a counselor, and a babysitter," Sara recalls.

Attending the sessions and talking with other adoptive parents was so helpful that Aaron decided they should go every year. Yet when the couple returned home, they found themselves feeling isolated and alone as summer arrived.

"I felt like our community had been ripped apart," Sara says about that time in their lives. "We live in a different state than our extended family, and I don't have a huge friend base here, especially a friend base that has done adoption."

The church the couple was attending had also fallen apart. "We were in the midst of finding a new church," Sara notes, "and I was kind of lost with God."

That's when life became especially stressful. Their young son, Luke, who was eventually diagnosed with fetal alcohol spectrum disorder, had been born with marijuana in his system. His birth mother had also used alcohol and narcotics at the time of his birth, and she had been diagnosed with schizophrenia and bipolar disorder.

Although the couple attempted to have an open adoption agreement with the birth mom, she often didn't make it to visitations. In fact, a judge hadn't formalized or signed the open adoption agreement, so legally the birth mom had no claim on Luke. Yet she told Sara and Aaron she wanted Luke back.

"This past summer, she started leaving weird messages on our phone that didn't make any sense," Sara says.

Not long after, the Department of Human Services called Sara to inform her that the birth mom had stolen guns from her grandparents' house.

"We don't know where she is," the official told Sara, "but we know she's stolen these guns and has threatened anybody who has anything to do with her kids' cases. So that means you need to go somewhere for a little while until we figure out what's going on."

Since it was summertime, Sara took her three children camping near their home while her husband went to work. That's when she checked Facebook and saw that the Refresh Summer Camp for adoptive families was happening that very weekend. The family drove eight hours to get there.

"It was definitely something that our family needed at the time, and God knew it and directed us there," Sara notes. "We just had this sense of relief and this sense of community with other people who had sympathy and understanding of our situation."

As Sara listened to an adoptive father speak at the camp, that sense of understanding helped her find God again.

"He said that when you're in the depths of the sea, you might think that God isn't there because you're drowning. But God cannot show you how He is performing in your life if everything is easy."

No longer in the "depths of the sea," Sara says she and her family are feeling safe again.

"We're in the shallow end again. I know the struggles aren't over, but I also know this: When you're in the depths of despair, God is there, and He won't let you drown."

Despite that situation and the difficulties their children's special needs present, this couple feels blessed by their kids.

"Every child is a child of God, and you have to have grace on them because they didn't choose this life," Sara points out. "They didn't choose to be affected by drugs. It's just as if I gave birth to them, and I was dealt the hand of a child with special needs. I would take that on. That is what God is giving me.

"It's definitely worth it. Their personalities click, they love each other, they play well together, and we have really good family times. My son cracks me up on a daily basis. He's such a joy to be around most of the time, and my girls are funny, smart, and artistic. I'm very proud of them."

Although it can be emotionally draining to deal with some aspects of her children's special needs, having a supportive community makes all the difference, she says.

"You need to have God in your life and a community to lift you up and say, 'Okay, you're not always going to be in the depth of the ocean. You also have this shallow end that's fun to play in.'"

🖊 Rest Stop

Our God is a triune God. He Himself is a community. If you're feeling resistant to the idea of being vulnerable and asking for support, ask God to reveal the joys and strength that a Christian community—the body of Christ—can supply. For the sake of your child, ask God to help you surrender any pride that may be keeping you from seeking help. Record your thoughts on your journal page.

My Journey to Adoption

DATE _____

Bear one another's burdens, and so fulfill the law of Christ.

Galatians 6:2

CHAPTER 7

Waiting

*Wait for the LORD; be strong, and let your heart
take courage; wait for the LORD!*

PSALM 27:14

I'll never forget waiting to meet Masha and Daniel (whose name
was Anatoliy at that time) at the Minneapolis airport. They were
flying in from Russia with other children from their orphanage and our adoption-agency staff. The agency had brought the
children to satisfy the first of two visits the Russian government
required as part of the adoption process.

My stomach had been churning for hours with intense excitement and anxiety—I'd never experienced any emotion quite like it.
It was late that December evening in 2002, and there was a crush
of people in the spot where we would meet them. We had sent this
nine- and ten-year-old sister and brother a photo of our family, but
we wondered what they would be thinking as they met us.

Suddenly, there they were. They were impossibly tiny for their
ages. Daniel looked exhausted, but his sister's smile was as wide
as the ocean they had just crossed. Masha clutched a photo in her

hand, crinkled and worn from much handling, and showed it to us. It was the photo we had sent them. Through the interpreter she said, "You look so happy in the picture!"

After accepting stuffed animals and bananas from us, the two slept in our van on the hour-long drive home. But when they entered our house, both were wide awake with excitement. The sight of our Christmas tree and the lights, the wrapped presents under the tree, and a pile of stuffed animals soon had them dancing around in delight. It wasn't long before they were laughing and playing with a pure joy I still vividly remember more than fourteen years later.

Daniel and Masha lived with us for three weeks, and then the unthinkable happened: They had to return to the orphanage in Russia. At the airport in January 2003, we were heartbroken to see Daniel sobbing while we said good-bye to these children who had become our own in such a short time.

After an interpreter told Daniel that we would see them in the spring when we visited them in Russia, he corrected the woman. "They aren't coming to visit," he said. "They're coming to bring us back home."

It was supposed to take two or three months for the Russian government to complete their part of the adoption paperwork and set a court date so we could travel to the orphanage and finalize the adoption. But we ended up waiting five long months before we were reunited with Daniel and Masha.

Waiting is difficult, but it often seems to be part of the process of adoption in one way or another. According to Kathy Ledesma, the national project director of AdoptUSKids, families considering adoption through the foster-care system "should plan on spending nine to 18 months, on average, to complete the inquiry, orientation, preparation classes . . . , and homestudy requirements. In 2014, children spent an average of 12 months in foster care between the time when parental rights were terminated and their adoption."[1]

If you're in a holding pattern as you read this, you're probably asking God why. While His ways are often a mystery, there are times when He does reveal Himself. Let's look at three stories and three ways God has worked during a waiting period.

SEEING GOD'S HEART

After Daniel and Masha boarded that plane for Russia, Jeff and I started waiting. Once a week, we would call the orphanage at 11:00 p.m. so we could speak to the kids at 8:00 a.m. their time. We didn't speak Russian, and Masha and Daniel couldn't speak English, but we thought it was important that they heard our voices and knew we hadn't forgotten them.

The phone calls weren't easy. It was painful to hear their little voices and know we couldn't be with them. One time Daniel kept saying a certain word over and over again: "*Skora? Skora?*" We thought he was saying "school" and assumed he had to get to class. Later, when we brought a Russian-speaking student to our home to translate for us, we learned he was saying, "Soon? Are you coming soon?"

Each week we would hang up the phone, and I would cry myself to sleep. We continued to wait . . . and wait. Then March 9, 2003, came, and I wrote this entry in my journal:

> *Last week was a roller coaster of emotions. We received our dossier with all of our documents and a list of things to bring to Russia. It made me feel as if we would soon be leaving. I even pulled out the suitcase and started packing Masha's and Anatoliy's clothes.*
>
> *Then we received an email saying our trip might be delayed until May. I was devastated! I felt physically*

crushed. I had to have a cry and pray and read my Bible.
I read the portion in John 17 where Jesus prays for all
believers. As I read, I realized just a bit of how much God
loves us. I thought of my pain of being separated from
Masha and Anatoliy—not knowing how they were, not
being able to help them, not being able to feed them well,
not knowing if they were safe from abuse.

I thought of God's separation from His children when
they turn their backs on Him and don't accept Him. The
pain I'm feeling now must be a taste of the pain and love
God feels for those who are apart from Him.

I was separated from my children by thousands of miles and bureaucratic red tape; God was separated from His children by sin and rebellion. At that time, God seemed to whisper to me, *I long to take My lost children in My arms just as you do with Masha and Anatoliy. But sometimes we have to wait.*

Near the end of John 17, Jesus says, "Father, I want those you have given me to be with me where I am" (verse 24, NIV). I certainly wanted my new children to be with me, but I felt stronger after God revealed more of Himself to me.

PREPARING OUR HEARTS

Kimberley Taylor also had to wait. "It had been a great mystery as to why God was allowing this adoption to take so long," she reflected. "It seemed to me that our baby would be better off with us, his new adoptive parents in the States, than in a Third-World country where there was no hope for him."[2]

During Kimberley's wait, her Bible-study group discussed 1 Corinthians 4:1: "Let a man regard us in this manner, as servants of Christ and stewards of the mysteries of God" (NASB). Kimberley says,

I pondered that verse during my study time but did not have an answer as to how it applied to me. As I met with my small group of women the next morning, I still did not have an answer to the question regarding the explanation of the mysteries of God. . . . We were deep into the lesson when the question came up, and the other women were equally puzzled. However, in an instant, God's spirit spoke to me and revealed my answer, saying, "During this delay I'm developing in you a mother's heart."[3]

Often, deciding to adopt through the foster-care system also becomes a lesson in waiting on God. It certainly was for Amy. She and her husband, Brian, already had three biological children and had adopted three children from two different countries when they became Gavin's foster parents in 2011. Even though they had experienced years of various adoption joys and struggles by that point, Amy said she was "naive" about the foster-care system.

The first phone call about their foster son proved that point.

"We have a baby boy for you," the social worker said.

"How old is he?"

"He is two days old."

Amy was excited. They had been praying for a son—and an infant.

"How long will we have him?"

"Oh, probably until he's eighteen," the social worker told her.

Amy immediately latched onto that answer, thinking, *Oh my goodness, God just gave us a son!*

Now that five years have passed, she realizes her assumption at the time was "very, very dangerous thinking in the foster-care world. I automatically thought we would be able to keep him forever."

In retrospect, Amy believes the social worker said what she did because the birth parents had developmental disabilities and weren't equipped mentally to care for their children.

Little did Amy know that she would battle anxiety as she and her husband waited four years before Gavin officially became their son in 2016. Gavin's birth father operated at the level of an eight-year-old, and the birth mom, who was later legally separated from the birth dad because she beat him, battled in court for four years for parental rights.

"They loved court because they got attention there," Amy says of the birth parents. "Going to court was a game for them. I was always on edge, always worried, and of course the Bible says to be anxious for nothing. When I first laid eyes on Gavin, it was like I gave birth to him—almost more so, because he was so helpless and alone."

Finally the birth parents terminated their parental rights voluntarily. But long before that happened, Amy had already decided to trust God with Gavin's future.

You love Gavin more than I love Gavin, she told God. *And You know exactly where he needs to be.*

Yet that trust didn't come easily or right away—it came through the waiting process.

"I was never mad at God. I just wanted it fixed," Amy notes. While she didn't shake her fist at God during that time, she *did* question the difficulty of the struggle.

Why doesn't God make it easier on me? she thought.

"I knew God was growing me spiritually, but I just wanted my selfish way. There's a reason for everything He does, so I try to go back to that."

In fact, during that long wait, God was preparing her heart to care for their next foster son (see that story in chapter 16).

WORKING HIS PLAN

In a *Focus on the Family* interview in 2016, Tricia Goyer shared that she had been praying for years about adoption before her husband, John, also felt God calling him to this step of faith. But when they submitted paperwork to adopt a baby girl from China, they discovered that the Chinese government decided to impose limits on American adoptions.

"I've been waiting years and years, God. I don't understand why You're closing the door now," Tricia thought. "I remember going to my room and just bawling my eyes out . . . but finally just relinquishing and saying, *God, this is my plan, a baby girl from China. Whatever . . . child or children You have for us—I just turn it over to You and I surrender to You. . . .* That afternoon . . . I got a call from a friend who knew a birth mom who was looking for a family to adopt her baby girl."[4]

The birth mom lived in the same town as the Goyers and was seven months pregnant. God did give the couple a baby girl—from the location *He* chose.

STILL WAITING?

If you're still waiting, it can be easy to feel as if God has forgotten you. If you feel this way, remember what the Lord said in Luke 12:6-7: "Are not five sparrows sold for two pennies? Yet not one of them is forgotten by God. Indeed, the very hairs of your head are all numbered. Don't be afraid; you are worth more than many sparrows" (NIV).

During my times of waiting, I've found Psalm 33:20 encouraging: "We wait in hope for the LORD; he is our help and our shield" (NIV). Reading every psalm that speaks of hope has strengthened me throughout periods of waiting, as has listening to Kathy Troccoli's song "I Wait."

Finally, consider the wise words of a godly Bible teacher

named Russell Kelfer, who wrote "Wait," a poem in which a child of God pleads with the Father to end an interminable, agonizing wait, and Kelfer imagines God's patient and loving answer. God's response details what this person would miss if the wait were to end too soon:

> *You would know that I give, and I save, for a start,*
> *But you'd not know the depth of the beat of My heart.*[5]

To know God's heart is a treasure worth the wait.

✏ *Rest Stop*

There are always seasons of life when we must wait, times when we don't know the outcome and feel in limbo. Ask God to help you be still before Him and wait patiently during your delay (Psalm 37:7). Does He want to reveal Himself to you? Does He want to develop something in your character or heart? Do you need to put aside your plans and surrender to His? After spending some time in prayer, record your thoughts on your journal page.

My Journey to Adoption

DATE _____

Lord, let me be like Noah, like Abraham, like David, who
waited and waited for Your timing and the fulfillment of
Your promises. They did not wait in vain, and neither do I.

From my journal, March 26, 2003

CHAPTER 8

Building Faith

My God will supply every need of yours according to his riches in glory in Christ Jesus.

PHILIPPIANS 4:19

As you welcome an orphan into your home in God's name, there is one truth you can rely on: God is faithful. He cares and provides for His children in so many ways.

Abraham was the first to call God "Jehovah-jireh" ("Jehovah will see and provide") after God supplied the ram for the sacrifice on Mount Moriah—but he wasn't the last person to do so!

While God provides for His people, He also clearly commands them to provide for orphans. Again and again throughout the Bible, we see how God cares for the fatherless and hear Him saying that His children must too. Deuteronomy 26:12-13, Psalm 146:9, and Isaiah 1:17, 23 are just a few of the many verses that reveal God's heart for orphans. God commands us to provide orphans with resources and justice. In fact, Deuteronomy 27:19 says, "Cursed be anyone who perverts the justice due to the sojourner, the fatherless, and the widow."

If God cares so deeply for orphans, you can be sure He will provide for you as you practice "religion that is pure and undefiled before God the Father" (James 1:27).

In Deuteronomy 14:29, God instructed the Israelites to tithe a portion of their produce to care for orphans (and widows, Levites, and immigrants). Do this, God told them, "that the LORD your God may bless you in all the work of your hands that you do."

Are you wondering how you'll be able to feed another mouth, find a vehicle to hold all of the kids, or deal with a child's possible disability? What if your child's behavior utterly baffles you and you don't know what to do? When these types of thoughts hang in our minds, we tend to forget that God provides. Even before a child enters your home, you may feel inadequate for the task and lacking what you need for the job. I certainly felt that way.

I'd had fourteen years of parenting experience, but as the date approached in 2003 when we would meet Masha and Daniel for the first time, I felt I was God's worst choice for this gig. As I ping-ponged between excitement and terror, I wrote this in my journal:

> I keep telling everyone that it's like getting a mystery
> package in the mail, except the mystery is wrapped in two
> human beings who need to be loved and taught. I can't
> figure out why God thinks I should be in on this. I feel so
> inadequate. I can be a nasty, selfish person. I'm not Mother
> of the Year. I've been too hard on Anna lately and had to
> apologize to her. Why me, Lord?

The beauty of the gospel is that Jesus died for us *knowing* we wouldn't have what it takes to be perfect. We sometimes forget that He doesn't *expect* us to do His will with only our minuscule abilities and resources. What He expects is that we become *dependent on Him*, because He is more than enough.

During my toughest moments, I've found God to be everything He says He is—faithful and true, my Provider, my Comforter, and more. He will never leave me—or you (Deuteronomy 31:6)—and He has provided the Holy Spirit to come alongside us, filling us with His power (Acts 1:8).

As you face the unknown in adoption and as a parent, know that God *will* provide for your family. In fact, He will often provide what you don't even know you need. Right now, your type-A personality might be telling you that you have everything under control, but God has plans to increase your dependence on Him through this adoption. You may be praying that God will heal your new child's heart and yet not realize He is planning to heal yours as well.

GOD LIKES SMALL

Adoptive mom Karly Leib remembers feeling ill equipped and overwhelmed at the prospect of adopting a child, even though she and her husband knew God was calling them to do so. To Karly, the obstacles seemed insurmountable—their house was too small, their car was too small, and their paycheck was definitely too small (her husband had left a lucrative position with a major corporation to work for a church). Even physical energy was lacking because they were already parenting three young children.

Why is God choosing us? she wondered.

She would have a hard day with her three children and think, *I can barely take care of these three. How will I take care of one more?*

She felt too inadequate, too small for the job, but God made it clear to Karly that He loves small.

"God reminded me of story after story in the Bible where

He called ill-equipped people to do His work," she says. "He did this so it would be apparent to all that it was God who was at work in and through His servants. People saw His work and were drawn to God again and again and put their faith in Him. He called Moses, who was afraid of public speaking, to confront Pharaoh and lead His people out of slavery. He called Gideon to rescue Israel from its wicked and powerful enemies, even though Gideon's clan was the weakest and he was the least in his family; later, God had Gideon shrink his army of thirty-two thousand men to three hundred before the army went out to fight, to make it clear that it was God who won the battle. And Jesus called Peter to be one of His disciples, even though Peter was just a regular fisherman.

"Through these stories, God helped me realize that He doesn't always choose the most qualified, likely-to-succeed people to do His work," Karly points out. "On the contrary, He is likely to do the opposite of that. He works like this, I realized, because He has different goals than we would if we were God. He is far more interested in people having an experience with Him than He is in getting a job done. God can get a job done anytime He wants. What He is really interested in is people knowing Him."

The Leibs came to know that God is faithful because He provided for them at each step of their adoption journey.

"If we had a big house and all the money we needed to adopt a child—and all the strength, energy, and patience required based on my own human effort—I would wind up patting myself on the back and feeling pretty proud of myself," Karly admits. "I wouldn't have needed anything from God on the journey, and so I probably wouldn't have turned to Him in faith. My weaknesses and hardships give God the opportunity to make His strength and His provision known. If God has called you to do something, then you don't need to worry about being qualified."

GOD'S BANK

God also provided for a midwestern couple in a dramatic and unmistakable way. Laura and her husband, Ed, were convinced that God was asking them to adopt another child.

"We thought, *Okay, we'll do this*," Laura says. "But we didn't have a dime."

They *did* own a piece of land on a small lake and had been trying to sell it to raise the money, but no one had shown interest. So the couple charged the adoption to their credit card. Then they borrowed money from friends and family and booked a flight to Russia to adopt a young boy. Yet they were troubled by doubt: *How are we going to pay for this? And are we doing the wrong thing?*

"The night before we flew to Russia, we were stressed out about the money. We needed a lot more to complete this adoption," Laura recalls. In the middle of the couple's anxious conversation, the phone rang. It was their real estate agent.

"Somebody wants your lake lot, and they want it now," he told them. "Before you leave tomorrow."

"I thought, *Huh? Are you kidding me?*" Laura admits.

Somehow the paperwork was completed that very evening, and the money from the sale was deposited in the bank.

"In my mind, this sudden sale was God saying, *Yes, this is the right thing to do. Here's the money.*"

God had cleared the way for Laura and Ed to fly out early the next morning.

I'VE GOT THIS

Over and over, God has provided financially for couples who follow His call to adopt a child.

After Jessamy and Jeff Johnson realized God was calling them to foster care, they proceeded—but slowly. Jessamy would have to give up her lucrative and fulfilling career that often took her away from home, and she and her husband, Jeff, had student loans to pay off.

While the couple was still waffling about the adoption decision, Jeff was in a car accident that totaled the vehicle but left him unscathed. The Johnsons knew there was a reason God protected him. That realization moved them to take action and obey the Lord, regardless of their finances.

Not long after that decision, Jessamy turned down a project paying six thousand dollars so she could be at home to care for a foster child. That happened on a Monday. On Tuesday, the couple received a check in the mail from their insurance company that covered the cost of their new car—*with six thousand dollars extra*.

Jessamy and Jeff heard God saying, *I told you to obey Me. I have this under control.*

The three siblings the couple adopted arrived just as Jessamy stopped earning money and Jeff was establishing his own business.

"The first year was rough financially," Jessamy says. "We even borrowed money from a relative. But my husband's salary literally doubled after the first year. God said over and over again, *If you're obedient, I'll take care of the rest.*"

PEACE OF MIND

God provides for our minds as much as our pocketbooks during the adoption process. He can dash our worldly worries and build our faith by providing His perspective—the only one that counts!

Adoptive mom Mandy Fiechtner experienced this as she sat with her new son in Ethiopia. After two months in that country, she was still waiting for adoption paperwork to be finalized while her husband and other son returned to their home in Washington State.

As she waited, she tried to teach this Ethiopian child some basic English. On this particular day, Mandy says the lesson ended up "with him in a fury and me fuming at the kitchen table."

As Mandy's frustrations spiraled, she shared them with God: *Really, God? You know if he can't speak English, he can't go to school, which means he won't graduate or go to college! He probably won't get married either!*

Mandy admits she basically overreacted during a stressful moment. "I had no idea of how to guide this eleven-year-old boy with so much history and yet so much ahead of him."

God heard her concerns—and answered immediately.

"For only the second or third time in my life, I heard God's voice loud and clear. And He said, *So what?*

"God went on to remind me that none of what I was worried about matters. And He challenged me with the reminder that He put this child in my life for one reason: that I might point him toward God. Everything else is simply an added bonus," Mandy says. "God made it clear that I need to make sure, above all else, that my children know the path to God so that if someday they choose to follow Him, the path will be easy to find."

At that moment, Mandy felt humbled . . . but also free from unnecessary worry. God's reminder to focus on the eternal gave her peace of mind as she and her new son faced the future.

EMOTIONAL HEALING

God may even surprise you with an emotional provision you never imagined. In her book *Choosing to See*, Mary Beth Chapman shares how God worked through an adoption to begin healing some pain from her own past.

The miracle happened as she and her husband, Steven Curtis Chapman, were in China waiting to meet their new baby girl.

Mary Beth was apprehensive. "It was like Satan was whispering in my ear that I . . . *couldn't* love this little girl the way she needed to be loved."[1] Yet as she walked through the door that led to her daughter, Mary Beth told God that she trusted Him. And when she saw the baby, she rushed to hold her. She writes,

> In that moment, time stopped. It was like God was speaking to me directly. "Mary Beth, you thickheaded woman, do you not understand now that this is the very way I see you? You are this orphan! I adopted you and you are Mine! I bought you for a price! Do you see how you love this baby? That's just a faint reflection of how much I love you! You didn't have a name, and I gave you a name. You did nothing to deserve [My] love, and I love you anyway. You had no hope, no future, and now you are the daughter of the *King*!"
>
> I saw it. The second she was placed in my arms, I would have fought to the death to protect her. I loved her with everything inside of me . . .
>
> [God] showed me the forever fierceness of *His* unconditional love for me, doing a work of grace in my life that I'd never known before.[2]

REST IN HIM

Throughout our lives, God will give us opportunities to learn to rest in His providence. Psalm 91:1 says, "He who dwells in the shelter of the Most High will remain secure and rest in the shadow of the Almighty [whose power no enemy can withstand]" (AMP). Yet we often do everything but rest and rely on our Provider. It can be so easy to forget that He has everything under control.

I remember having a stressful day with Daniel during our first year together. Because of his traumatic background, he presented many behaviors that were hard for Jeff and me to understand and difficult to live with. Feeling at a loss and like a failure at this new kind of parenting, I left the house for the privacy of our rural yard and stood alone under the evening stars.

"I can't do this, God!" I cried. "How can I help him? I'm lousy at this!"

God replied, *Are you doing this alone?*

His words stopped me in my tracks. How could I forget that Jehovah-jireh could supply the wisdom, strength, resources, and anything else I needed? How could I forget that the almighty God—the Alpha and the Omega, who is and who was and who is to come—was with me?

When you face a need, remember the One who is faithful and true, the One who rescued you, the One who adopted you, the One who did not leave *you* as an orphan either (John 14:18).

✐ Rest Stop

Meditate on 2 Corinthians 9:8: "God is able to make all grace abound to you, so that having all sufficiency in all things at all times, you may abound in every good work." What provision do you need from God in this moment? Ask your faithful Provider to supply what you need for today. On your journal page, keep a record of your requests and how God answers them.

My Journey to Adoption

DATE _____

Let us hold unswervingly to the hope we
profess, for he who promised is faithful.

Hebrews 10:23, NIV

CHAPTER 9

Foster-Care Challenges

As we share abundantly in Christ's sufferings, so through
Christ we share abundantly in comfort too.

2 CORINTHIANS 1:5.

Your eyes will behold the king in his beauty.

ISAIAH 33:17

Most of the world doesn't see a connection between suffering and beauty. Yet on the cross, Jesus gave us the supreme example of how these polar opposites can form an alliance.

What does this have to do with the foster-care system in this country? If you've researched this path to adoption, you know it's not always an easy one. If you enter the system, you're likely to suffer from its rules and regulations, the vagaries of a social worker's decisions, the uncertainty and anxiety of waiting for parental rights to be terminated, difficult visits with birth parents, or other complications.

That's not to say that adoption can't happen quickly through the foster-care system. It can; it's all up to God's plan. And special relationships with birth parents that benefit your children are possible too. One couple's child recently took part in his birth dad's wedding, and all rejoiced that this man had become a Christian.

But as you enter the foreign world of this understaffed government program, run by fallible, overworked human beings, know that suffering can come.

"A social worker's job has become a paper-pushing job," says D. J. Jordan, who served on the Virginia State Board of Social Services, which oversees the foster-care system in that state. "They see things that will make you cry, and then they have to go back to work and see it again the next day."[1]

Jordan, an adoptive and foster father, reminds people to have patience with social workers and to pray for them. If you face hard situations as you work with the foster-care system, remember that God has a plan. Watch for His beauty, even in painful circumstances.

A GREAT GIFT

After hearing a Francis Chan sermon that convinced them to surrender everything to God—even their comfort—Robbie and Karly Leib sensed God calling them to adopt a child (see chapter 5 for this part of their story). Through the death of their dear friends' son, God helped them realize that only He knows how many days, months, or years parents have with a child. That truth gave the couple great peace as they became foster parents.

Less than two weeks after their friends' son died, a social worker asked the Leibs to take in a baby boy who had been born that day. The infant was entering care because of his birth mom's history with the department.

"We don't know if you'll have him two days, two months, two years, or the rest of his life," the social worker told them.

"Robbie and I just assumed we would get an older child," Karly says. "But when they told us about this baby boy, we both knew we were supposed to say yes."

From day one, Karly realized that loving the little boy would be easy. "The minute they put JJ in my arms at the hospital, I was his mama. I had the same love in my heart for him that I did when my other three children were born."

Because of this, Karly immediately knew that losing this little boy would be unbearable. Her mind began to fill with anxious thoughts. *How could I ever survive losing this precious baby? How could I bear losing my son?*

It was during those times of fear that God taught Karly to pray the Garden Prayer. It was the prayer Jesus himself had prayed the night before He was crucified. Knowing how greatly He would suffer, Jesus was still able to pray these words of surrender in the garden of Gethsemane: "Father, if you are willing, take this cup from me; yet not my will, but yours be done" (Luke 22:42, NIV).

When fear would grip her, Karly learned to pray as Jesus did: *Lord, we desperately want to keep JJ. Yet not our will but Your will be done.*

Still, every day was a battle; every day she had to choose to live fearfully or faithfully. After JJ had been in the Leibs' home four months, Karly wrote this journal entry as she struggled with the unknown:

> *One day we will know where JJ is going to stay and grow up, and all this waiting will be over. Then I will look back and read these words and recognize that God had a plan all along.*
>
> *Job 26:7 says, "He suspends the earth over nothing" (NIV). The Lord upholds my life, and JJ's life, and his mom's life. We are resting in His powerful, mighty hands. The same hands that are holding up the earth in its place in the universe are holding me up.*

What is there to fear? Do I fear that He will drop the earth? And if not, why would I fear that He would drop me? Or that He would let go of JJ? How much harder is it to hold up a planet than one person, or one family? Where is my faith?

Lord, You have blessed us with this precious boy for sixteen weeks. Every day with him is a gift from You. You brought him to us in Your perfect wisdom and love. You know how this story ends. You know where JJ will end up. But for now it is Your will that he remains with me, in my arms, in my home, in my heart.

Around the time JJ was seven months old, his birth mom started missing visits with him or left visits early. She also stopped regularly doing what the court had mandated if she were to regain custody. And then she disappeared. No one knew where she was, and there was no indication that she was coming back.

"We were worried for his mom and asked everyone on our prayer team to pray for her," Karly says. "But at the same time, we were hopeful that this would mean our son would get to stay with the only family he had ever lived with."

After more than three months passed with no word from the birth mom, a petition was filed to terminate parental rights.

Even if she does come back, it will be too late, Karly thought. *JJ will stay with us where he belongs!*

SURRENDERING AGAIN

Then one day, JJ's birth mom returned. She wanted another chance. "I had mistakenly believed the journey was over," Karly admits.

Suddenly the Leibs' one-year-old son was forced to attend visits with his birth mom again—a complete stranger to him by then. Karly's emotions vacillated between anger toward JJ's mom and pity for her. The woman was pregnant again, and her son didn't want anything to do with her. Karly knew that being Christlike meant forgiving this woman and showing her grace and compassion. But this was easier said than done.

From the beginning of JJ's placement, the Leibs had prayed for his mom's salvation, and they also asked friends and family to pray for her. But the longer the foster-care case wore on with no resolution, the more Karly struggled to pray that prayer honestly.

"I vividly remember one time—after JJ had been with us for more than a year—when I was feeling convicted that I should be praying for the birth mom's salvation. I knew how double-minded I was. I didn't want to pray that prayer because I was afraid her salvation would lead to us losing JJ. I confessed this mental struggle to the Lord, and right away I felt Him asking me, *Would you send her to hell so you could keep JJ? Or would you choose her salvation, even if it meant losing your son?*"

In that moment, Karly knew she must choose the woman's salvation. Here was the suffering and sacrifice Pastor Chan had talked about. Here also was the beauty of Christ. After Karly once more surrendered her desires to Jesus, she committed to praying for a miracle in the birth mom's heart—and the miracle occurred! JJ's mom accepted Jesus Christ as her Lord and has been walking faithfully with Him for several years.

"Our God is so big!" Karly says. "He's so loving and merciful, and His plans are so much higher than ours. When we began this ministry, we thought God was calling us to rescue a little boy. But after seeing the amazing transformation take place in JJ's mom, we finally realized that God's plan all along had been to rescue a whole family. By the grace of God, we were able to accept that His plan was better."

THE LAST NIGHT

On her last night with JJ, after two and a half years of mothering this little boy, Karly sent this email to the family's prayer team:

> *Tonight I tucked in my precious boy for the last time as his mommy. Oh that baby! He has been such a gift! He has brought so much joy to our lives. It is hard to imagine what our lives will be like without him.*
>
> *Tomorrow morning we will leave early to take him to his mama's house. It's going to be a special time, and we are choosing to think of it as a celebration of a family reunited. My parents will be there, and so will all of our kids, plus a few people from the birth mom's church who want to pray for all of us. I think it's going to give us a good feeling of closure. We are rejoicing in the work that God has done in his birth mom's life, and we are turning our thoughts to reflect on her joy.*
>
> *This journey with JJ has taught us that God is enough. He has been worthy, every step of the way, of our trust. He answered all of our prayers in His own perfect way. He has asked us to sacrifice so much for JJ. But He sacrificed first when He gave His own Son to save us.*
>
> *Our God didn't stand far off watching us suffer. Instead, He entered into our suffering and took all of our sin and shame to the cross, so that one day we will suffer no more— for eternity.*
>
> *It's this truth that keeps us going. It's the knowledge of God's sacrifice and great love that empowers us so that even now we know we will do this again. Our prayer is that our story, JJ's story, would cause you to worship God. This is for His glory. Lord, Your will be done on earth as it is in heaven. Amen.*

The Leibs gave JJ and his family a great gift at a high cost to themselves. They learned what it means to suffer for the sake of Christ and live out the gospel, and they also saw the beauty of God's unlimited, unconditional love.

"We are just so thankful that God chose us to be a part of His story of redemption and reconciliation," Karly says.

BE FAITHFUL

No one wants to love and care for an infant for two years and then have to give him away. It goes against every fiber of a parent's being. So it makes sense that couples considering adoption through the foster-care system fear that possible loss. And if you must let a child go, you certainly aren't guaranteed a salvation story.

While it's only human to want a happy ending and to pray for it, it's dangerous to believe we only need to follow a formula to obtain it. If we believe that, we're deceiving ourselves. We're telling ourselves that we're in control, not God.

We must give the beginnings, the middles, and the endings to the Lord. We must concentrate on being faithful to God no matter the outcome—whether we're able to adopt a certain child or not, whether a child we adopt ends up having bipolar disorder, grows up to work in ministry, makes us proud grandparents, or struggles with addiction.

In God's eyes, the people listed in Hebrews 11 were heroes of the faith. These people were faithful no matter what God asked them to do, no matter how dire the circumstances were, no matter what the outcome would be. While some heroes saw miracles, others did not. From our earthly viewpoint, the believers listed in verses 35-38 didn't have what we would call a happy, successful ending:

Some were tortured, refusing to accept release, so
that they might rise again to a better life. Others

suffered mocking and flogging, and even chains and imprisonment. They were stoned, they were sawn in two, they were killed with the sword. They went about in skins of sheep and goats, destitute, afflicted, mistreated—of whom the world was not worthy— wandering about in deserts and mountains, and in dens and caves of the earth.

All these people were commended for their faith. From God's viewpoint, these tortured believers—the ones who were stoned and sawed in two—*were* successful because of their faithfulness to Him.

I imagine many parents feel as if they're being sawed in two if they must let a child they love live with someone else. It sure isn't the ending they had envisioned. But the Leibs, and many families like them, are continuing in their faith and loving God no matter the outcome. You won't see these families being applauded like sport stars in an auditorium of fans, but you can be sure that God and His angels are singing their praises and adding them to a heavenly list of Hebrews 11 heroes.

Aim to be faithful to God as you adopt from the foster-care system, and surrender your will to His. We read in Habakkuk 2:4 that "the righteous shall live by his faith." It may be that God will allow you to raise your foster child to adulthood. On the other hand, He may want you to serve as a temporary intercessor. That was the case for Rosaria and Kent Butterfield when they welcomed a newborn girl into their home in 2007 with plans to adopt her.

EMBRACE THE RISK

In her book *The Secret Thoughts of an Unlikely Convert*, Rosaria shares that ten days after she and her husband brought the baby home, a government director disrupted the adoption process because she disagreed with placing an African-American baby in a Caucasian family.

The Butterfields didn't want the baby languishing in the foster-care system during a court case, so they decided against launching a legal battle. Instead, they prayed that the baby would have a Christian home. As they faced the last day with the little girl, they wondered if they had made the right decision.

"The day that was S's last one with us was dark and fearful," Rosaria writes. "We tearfully brought S back to the agency, and there we met S's preferred potential adoptive family. They were African-American and Christian. God heard our prayers. Yes, we were hurt. Deeply. But S wasn't! In God's amazing mercy, He used us to protect the baby!"[2]

A year later, as Rosaria and her pastor-husband officiated at a worship service, a family walked in with a girl. It was Baby S. The mom put S in Rosaria's arms, and without thinking, Rosaria carried her to the front of the church to lead the singing of Psalm 78.

"Kent was reading from the book of Exodus," writes Rosaria. "He was retelling the story of Moses' parents placing him in a basket of reeds, lowering him into the Nile, not knowing his destination. I handed Kent Baby S as I flipped through the Psalter. . . . Kent embraced the baby in his arms, and mouthed, 'Who is this?' I told him, and he broke into tears."[3]

I'm sure it was no coincidence that Kent Butterfield was reading those particular verses in Exodus when the infant they had given to God "by faith" a year earlier was placed in his arms. There are parents in the Bible who also "by faith" gave up children for God: "By faith Moses' parents hid him for three months after he was born, because they saw he was no ordinary child, and they were not afraid of the king's edict" (Hebrews 11:23, NIV). Moses's parents risked their lives for a child they sensed God had set apart, in the end allowing someone else to raise their son.

Hebrews 11:17 records Abraham's act of faith—his willingness to obey God and offer his promised, one-and-only son as a sacrifice. This wasn't the first time Abraham had to act in faith. Long before, God had told him to leave his home, and Abraham obeyed, "even though he did not know where he was going" (verse 8, NIV).

In one of his Bible commentaries, Matthew Henry noted that even though the faithful "know not always their way, yet they know their guide, and this satisfies them."[4]

As you commit to adopting a child from the foster-care system, know that you are following the heroes of faith. Like Abraham, you may not know the destination of your journey, but you will be following in Christ's footsteps, risking pain for the beauty of the Cross and the commendation of God.

As you go, find encouragement in Charles Spurgeon's wise words concerning trials and faith, suffering and beauty:

> We would never know the music of the harp if the strings
> were left untouched or enjoy the juice of the grape if it
> were not trodden in the winepress or discover the sweet
> perfume of cinnamon if it were not pressed and beaten
> or feel the warmth of fire if the coals were not utterly
> consumed. The wisdom and power of the great Workman
> are discovered by the trials through which His vessels of
> mercy are permitted to pass. Present afflictions tend also
> to heighten future joy. There must be shadows in the
> picture to bring out the beauty of the light.[5]

Rest Stop

Read Hebrews 11 and ask God to help you be faithful as you pursue adoption through the foster-care system. Record your thoughts on your journal page.

My Journey to Adoption

DATE _____

[Noah's] faith influenced his practice. . . . He did not dispute
with God why he should make an ark, nor how it could be
capable of containing what was to be lodged in it, nor how
such a vessel could possibly weather out so great a storm. His
faith silenced all objections, and set him to work in earnest.

Matthew Henry's commentary on the book of Hebrews

PART 3

At Home

CHAPTER 10

Loving like Jesus

*This is my commandment, that you love
one another as I have loved you.*

JOHN 15:12

It's common for prospective adoptive parents to ask themselves, "Will we be able to love a child we adopt?" When a couple poses that question, they're usually wondering if they will feel an instant emotional bond or connection with their new child. There are two answers to that question.

Yes, some parents may feel a bond with their new child in a short amount of time. Some stories in this book have described women who felt an instant bond to a child they adopted with their husbands. And no, many parents don't feel an instant bond with the child they adopt, no matter the child's age.

If you aren't feeling emotionally connected to the child you've adopted, know that this isn't unusual. It's not your fault; you are not a "bad" parent. It often takes time to develop *feelings* of love.

"Not once . . . had I given a single thought to the idea that it would also be *me* who would need to feel bonded with *her*," says one adoptive father. "I didn't know that bonding was a two-way street. I'd just assumed that after we received our referral packet and I saw my daughter's cute little face, knew her name and that she needed a mom and dad, I would be automatically and instantly bonded with her."[1]

There's a solution to this dilemma. It's spelled out in 1 Corinthians 13:4-7:

> Love is patient and kind; love does not envy or boast; it is
> not arrogant or rude. It does not insist on its own way; it is
> not irritable or resentful; it does not rejoice at wrongdoing,
> but rejoices with the truth. Love bears all things, believes
> all things, hopes all things, endures all things.

This definition doesn't say that love is an instant emotional connection with someone. Of course, we *want* to develop an emotional bond with our new children—that desire is natural. God even gave us brain chemicals that help us bond to our children. Oxytocin, for example, is a hormone released during childbirth and breastfeeding to facilitate bonding.[2]

We can encourage bonding in many ways, but until a bond is developed, we'll need to operate solely on an unconditional Jesus kind of love—love that's an action, not just a feeling.

You may need to love a child who may seem like a stranger, or even worse, a very unpleasant stranger who treats you in a nasty way or screams for an hour straight. Don't give up. Love the child with your actions, knowing that for a time you may need to love selflessly without receiving much in return.

LOVING A STRANGER

Marlene Molewyk expected to instantly fall in love with the eighteen-month-old girl she and her husband adopted, even though her social worker warned her that acquiring this motherly feeling toward the toddler might take time.

The social worker explained, "Just imagine walking down the street, picking out some random kid, and bringing her home to be your daughter. That's what it's going to feel like for you and your adopted child. You're essentially parenting a complete stranger who will feel like she's just been kidnapped. So here's the advice I give to all adoptive parents: Fake it till you make it. Act like you love your adopted daughter, because she really needs this from you. Eventually your emotions will follow your actions."

When Marlene's daughter Anna came home, the little girl was happy whenever friends came to visit. "But as soon as they left, Anna became sullen and defiant. She fought with her new siblings and tore little holes in the walls all throughout the house," Marlene says. She also frequently and deliberately disobeyed her new mother and then glared at her.

"Over time, I felt increasingly angry and annoyed at her," Marlene recalls. "I had to continuously remind myself, *She's just a toddler who's acting out because she's scared and upset about being taken away from everyone and everything she knows. Cut the poor kid a break!*"

Then one afternoon Marlene discovered a huge puddle of Elmer's glue on the carpet. Thinking Anna had done this, Marlene felt incredibly angry. But just a few minutes later, she discovered that one of her biological daughters was the real culprit, and to her surprise, the anger disappeared.

"This really bothered me," Marlene admits, "because it showed me exactly where my heart was toward Anna. I realized I didn't love her the way I loved my biological children, and to be completely honest, I wasn't sure that I loved her at all."

This kindhearted, compassionate Christian woman berated

herself and then decided she was a poor excuse for a Christian. That's when her husband reminded her of the "fake it till you make it" advice.

"With this in mind, I hugged Anna, kissed her, and acted as loving as I possibly could toward her," Marlene says. "And after several years, I'm glad to report that my emotions finally did follow my actions. It has now been eight years since the adoption, and I love Anna with the same fierce, all-encompassing, protective love I feel toward my biological children. I'm very thankful that she is part of our family, which would not be complete without her."

ON EMPTY

Unfortunately, many parents are caught off guard when the "instant" love they were counting on doesn't occur.

Irene Garcia remembers how ashamed she was when she realized she felt absolutely no love for Joe, a nine-year-old boy she and her husband, Domingo, were adopting. Love came easily when Irene gave birth to her first child. "It was instant and breathtaking," she recalls. And when she and Domingo adopted a baby girl, she instantly felt love for her also.

"But here was a boy who was going to be my son, and I was empty, void of any good feelings," she says. "I wasn't prepared for the guilt that overtook my heart. I was ashamed."

Joe's habits irritated Irene. He had an insatiable hunger, and he would steal food not just at home but wherever they went. She would always find food in his pockets.

"He would shove food in his mouth just to annoy me. He knew this made me crazy inside."

One day Irene looked out the kitchen window and saw Joe facedown in the pool. She panicked and screamed as she ran outside. Then he lifted his head and started laughing. "At that moment I felt that if there was any love in me for him, it was poured out. After that day I was on empty and couldn't muster any feelings toward him."

Domingo reminded his wife that she needed to provide love with her actions, without expecting a flood of emotions.

"When you adopt older kids, it's tough," she explains. "We need to be honest with one another and share these things. Like my husband reminded me, love is an action. The feeling isn't always there, but the action covers us. Adopting older kids is life changing because you realize we are totally dependent on God and His grace."

Four years later, as she and two of her daughters boarded a bus for a Christian camp, Irene felt differently about Joe as she said good-bye to him.

"Oh, how I'd learned to love this animated and charismatic child," Irene writes in her book *Rich in Love*. "Domingo's words suddenly echoed in my mind. He had been right. The act of loving Joseph with God's agape love had turned into a flooding emotion. This was my boy, and I loved him with all my heart."[3]

At the camp, she opened her suitcase and found a note from Joe inside, saying how much he loved her and thanking her for his new life.

"I've learned love comes from Jesus, and it's supernatural," says Irene, who went on to adopt and foster many older children with her husband. "I don't always *feel* it, but I can *be* it. I can serve, care, and meet the needs of my children. I can do the things God has called me to do. My feelings will come and go, but I will no longer feel the guilt and shame I once felt. I will always remember that my love is not overflowing, but God's love is. I will continually be on my knees asking Him to fill me up with His love so I can pass it on to others, especially my kids."

TWO LOVE LESSONS

As with Irene, God deepened my understanding of His love through adoption. I'll never forget Daniel and Masha's second night in our home. I went to bed feeling scared. Daniel seemed to have this tough exterior and wouldn't look at me. Masha was cute but was a stranger to me. Would I be able to love these children as much as my biological kids?

Lord, I prayed that night, *help me to love these children. Give me Your love for them.*

LESSON 1: GOD'S LOVE IS LIMITLESS

On one of our first days together, my husband and I took Masha and Daniel shopping for clothes and then asked if there was anything special they would like.

"Balloons!" Daniel said immediately.

He and Masha blew them up with an excitement you'd usually see in much younger kids. They drew faces on the balloons, tied string to them, hit them about, rubbed them in their hair, and laughed and laughed.

We later learned there was a special kind of balloon that Daniel wanted very much: the kind that stays afloat in the air. His dream came true after we ate at a restaurant that just happened to be giving away helium balloons.

When Daniel held that balloon in his hands, the look of joy on his face was exquisite. As we stepped outside into the cold winter air, he bounced the balloon around and gazed at it, holding it by the very end of the ribbon that kept it tied to the earth. I motioned for him to be careful and then realized that Daniel wanted to let go of his treasure. With body language and facial expressions, this eleven-year-old Russian boy asked me if he could release it.

He just received it, I thought, *and now he wants to watch it fly away?*

With my approval, he let the ribbon slip from his fingers, and we both watched the purple oval float into the gray winter sky. With our eyes, we followed the balloon for a long time while it drifted up and up, proving to us how wide and high the earth's atmosphere really is. It's easier to grasp the enormity of the sky when you watch something disappear into its vastness.

There is something even larger than the sky—the love of Christ. I knew this because God had proved it to me. Eighteen days after asking Jesus to help me love Masha and Daniel, I wrote this:

> *I am now unequivocally and madly in love with these gifts from above. The infinite nature of God's love amazes me. We think we cannot possibly love another person, or care about someone else, or help one more neighbor in need. But God has other plans, and more than enough love to pour into our hearts. I'm reminded of this passage: "I pray that you, being rooted and established in love, may have power, together with all the Lord's holy people, to grasp how wide and long and high and deep is the love of Christ" (Ephesians 3:17-18, NIV).*
>
> *Like Daniel letting go of his balloon, my husband and I released our well-ordered life when we said yes to adoption. Now, just as Daniel did, we are looking toward the heavens with delight.*

LESSON 2: LOVE INVOLVES SACRIFICE

A few months after the adoption was finalized, we began to see another side of Daniel. This handsome little boy with a dark complexion and a mischievous smile was always waiting for something bad to happen. After all, that was the pattern of his life—very bad things happened to him on a regular basis. He was afraid of what would happen next, but his fear came out as anger, usually toward me. Those first few months might have been easier had I understood this right from the beginning. Unfortunately, it took me a while to figure it out.

One morning after hearing an annoyed tone in my voice as I tried to hurry Masha to get ready for school, he yelled, "You kick us! You hurt us!"

I was doing no such thing, so his pronouncement upset me. It wasn't until I later spoke to his therapist that I began to understand that my tone of voice must have triggered memories of earlier abuse in Daniel's mind.

But that morning I was angry. Why was he accusing me of hurting him? Why was he always so mad at me and so difficult? I'd done nothing but care for his every need for months, to the point of exhaustion!

Daniel hadn't wanted to go to school that day. First he had declared, "I'm not going to eat. I'm not going to take a snack." Then when it was time to leave, he told me, "I don't have time to eat! I need a snack!" His oppositional behavior was frustrating.

It's embarrassing now to see that I was offended by this little boy's words and that part of my heart was expecting better treatment because of my care for him. After I managed to wrangle Daniel and Masha to school, I studied my Bible and prayed. *God, it hurts that Daniel is saying these things—these lies—saying that I kicked him! It hurts to be the target of his rage when I saved him from the orphanage, when I changed my whole life for him!*

I was so selfishly wrapped up in my own emotions that I didn't realize the irony of my statements. This was the moment when God gently taught His clueless daughter another love lesson.

I know how you feel, He gently whispered to my spirit. *I saved you. I gave up My life for you, and I took a lot of pain while doing it. You're taking his pain. Keep loving him like I love you.*

In that moment, I felt the depth of God's love for me as never before. I was overwhelmed with Jesus' sacrifice for me. His love for me flowed into my soul, helping me love Daniel in a deeper way.

The next time Daniel flashed back to his earlier life of abuse, I was able to respond differently. He often punished himself by not eating, and one night he wouldn't come to supper. I think the early neglect had something to do with this.

As I told him to come and eat before I put the food away, he started screaming, "You don't feed me! You're a bad mom! I'll be hungry!" He tried to run out the front door—he had run away several times already—but I hugged him, and we ended up sitting on the floor in front of the door.

With my arms still wrapped around this skinny boy, I asked him, "Daniel, what's the truth? The truth is, I'm not your Russian mother. The truth is that I feed you, right? Is there food on the table right now?"

As I helped him focus on the truth of his new life instead of the trauma of his past life, he calmed down and then ate his supper. I, too, was reminded to focus on the truth of God instead of Satan's lies as I learned how to love my son unconditionally. It's not easy to respond day after day with agape love, and I certainly failed more times than I'd like to mention.

Most people won't understand anything about loving a child with a traumatic past, which can be difficult. A wise adoptive mom from the West Coast didn't let this misunderstanding bother her one day while she was at her son's school conference. A teacher with tears in her eyes looked at this mom and said, "I feel so bad for you. When your son wrote his paper about being thankful, it was about his birth mom. That must break your heart."

But this mother didn't cry. She cheered! She was overjoyed

that her son was able to share his emotions in this way since the past year of therapy had focused on helping him express his feelings. That's agape love!

MORE THAN LOVE

Doing your best to love like Jesus will go a long way toward helping your new child, but children who have been wounded will need more than your love. They will need your patient endurance and understanding, your knowledge of trauma-informed parenting, your humbleness, and your willingness to find additional support and do what's necessary to help them heal.

In a *Focus on the Family* interview, adoptive father John Goyer said he realized that caring for a child from the foster-care system would be more difficult than what he and his wife, Tricia, had experienced as they raised their biological children.

"But I still wasn't ready for what came. . . . It's not enough just to say 'I love you and I'm here for you,'" he explained. "It takes a lot of therapy. It took a lot of time. And really it took a lot of . . . patience, working through the baggage that's in their [lives]." John added,

> [Now] I have a new appreciation for my heavenly Father. When [my child was] having a screaming rage and I had to hold [her] in my arms, that would sometimes go on for an hour. And the whole time I'm just softly telling her, "We can't act like this; this isn't appropriate. But I still love you, and you're still my forever little girl."
>
> And as I would tell her that, I could hear the heavenly Father speaking that to me, 'cause I'm not perfect and I've made lots of mistakes. And He'd say, "There's consequences for your actions, but I still love you, and you're My forever son."[4]

If you expect to form an instant bond with your child, you may be disappointed. Don't be. Just begin to be Jesus with skin on, and as you do, ask God to pour some of His infinite love into your heart so it can flow out to your son or daughter. God's love never disappoints!

Rest Stop

What actions can you take today to show a Jesus kind of love to your child or someone else? Is there something you need to bear, believe, hope, or endure in the name of Jesus and His love? Take time to pray, and then record your thoughts on the journal page.

My Journey to Adoption

DATE _____

In the New Testament, love is more of a verb than
it is a noun. It has more to do with acting than with
feeling. The call to love is not so much a call to a
certain state of feeling as it is to a quality of action.

R. C. Sproul, *Discovering the Intimate Marriage*

CHAPTER 11

Joy and Grief

*Be glad in the LORD, and rejoice, O righteous,
and shout for joy, all you upright in heart!*

PSALM 32:11

*Though [God] cause grief, he will have compassion
according to the abundance of his steadfast love.*

LAMENTATIONS 3:32

We're more than ready for the joy of welcoming children into our lives, but are we also prepared for grief?

The Bible makes it clear that there is a time for grief—it's a part of life and a natural process (Ecclesiastes 3:4). All of Israel mourned for thirty days when Aaron and Moses died. The Hebrew people grieved by wailing, crying out in loud voices, cutting slits in their clothing, and sitting in silence on the ground.

In our fast-moving society, we're more apt to overlook this process. But shouldn't we expect little children who have lost a parent to mourn? Shouldn't we expect a child who has been hurt to respond to that pain and any losses connected to it?

It's important to recognize that some of your child's behaviors could be an expression of grief. And you may also find yourself grieving as you learn the hard details of your child's past and witness his or her pain.

The good news is this: Jesus—the man acquainted with sorrow yet filled with joy more than all others—can turn ashes to beauty, mourning to joy, and despair to praise (Isaiah 61:3). That's the truth we need to claim and teach our children as we allow them to grieve their losses.

GRIEF

As I grieved a death in my family, I thought of Daniel's and Masha's world-altering losses and wondered how they had survived. How could a two- and three-year-old process the loss of a father, and later at ages six and seven, the loss of their mother, grandparents, half siblings, and everyone else they knew as they were hauled off to an orphanage hundreds of miles away? They were tossed into an institutional setting, surrounded by strangers, and they never saw a relative again.

I, on the other hand, was fifty-two at the time of my loved one's death and had the support of my family, church, Christian coworkers, and God, who sustained me during this loss. Still, the loss was hard. I cannot grasp the depth of grief my kids must have experienced.

Your child won't have the same experiences, but no matter when, where, or how a child loses a parent, there is grief. The initial loss of a mother and father may be compounded by additional losses, such as the loss of typical childhood experiences, comfort items, special foods, or a sense of security because of multiple moves from foster home to foster home.

Children also may grieve what they can't remember. There might not be anyone to fill in the details, to talk about the day they were born or tell funny stories about what they were like as toddlers.

Following are six important steps for helping a child work through grief:

1. RECOGNIZE IT

The danger for us as adoptive parents is not recognizing a child's grief. But we can look for it, keeping in mind that grief can show up in various ways throughout the different stages of childhood as understanding and perspective grow along with our children's bodies.

Among other behaviors, a younger child may show grief by wetting the bed, throwing temper tantrums, being destructive, or complaining of constant stomachaches or other ailments. Older kids may not be able to concentrate on schoolwork or remember your instructions. They may even run away or become withdrawn. Your new child may also be irritable, cry for hours, or need to sleep next to you for a month.

Anyone who has lost someone knows the truth of C. S. Lewis's observation: "Grief is like a long valley, a winding valley where any bend may reveal a totally new landscape."[2] That new landscape for your child may come on a holiday—Mother's Day, Father's Day, Christmas, or an anniversary of a life event. Grief may be triggered by school assignments requiring a family tree or baby photos that don't exist, by the changes of puberty, or as an older teen grapples with issues of identity.

> **IDENTITY QUESTIONS MANY ADOPTED ADOLESCENTS ASK[1]**
>
> - Who am I? Am I like my adoptive parents or my birth parents or both?
> - I know little about my birth parents, so how can I possibly figure out who I am?
> - What does it mean that I'm Hispanic? Korean? African American?
> - Whom would I have been if I had stayed with my birth family?
> - Would life have been different for me?
> - What would have been different about me?

Do what you can to help your child express and process the grief, whether that's answering questions, validating your child's losses, providing your presence and comfort, or simply crying along with your child.

If children are old enough, you can help them name their feelings and understand that their emotions are normal. To do this with my kids, I placed a chart on our kitchen wall of various facial expressions along with the words describing the emotions.

Grief can sometimes be expressed as anger. So if Daniel was feeling angry (which was often), I could point to the chart and ask him if he had any other feelings. Was he sad? Afraid? Worried? An emotions chart, which you can find online, can give your child words for what's happening on the inside.

2. ALLOW IT

Allow your child a special time to grieve. When Daniel began sharing painful memories, we used what we called the Mad Box. Maybe calling it a Sad Box would work better for your child. For us, placing something representative of Daniel's anger (and the underlying grief) inside the box as we talked about it was a way to help him begin processing his emotions.

My friend made beautiful wooden boxes for my two kids; Daniel's box featured Spider-Man on the cover, his favorite superhero. The first item he placed in his Mad Box was a stick symbolizing the times his mother had beaten him with a branch of a bush that made his skin itch.

One Saturday afternoon, Daniel became agitated after he followed me into my bedroom and noticed I was crying.

"These are happy tears," I told him. I was reading an old love letter from my husband, and it was a good memory.

Daniel had never seen "happy" tears, so he was skeptical, and his anxiety grew. As our therapist suggested, I began asking him questions about his body to help him understand his feelings. "Is your stomach tight?" "Does your head hurt?" "Why do you feel bad?" "Did your birth mom cry a lot?"

"Yes, she cried a lot," he said. Then he asked if he could be mad at her.

We talked about that for a while as I let him know his feelings were normal. Any little boy would be angry and sad that his mother had disappeared, I explained. I stressed that it wasn't his fault that his mother left. And then he shared another painful memory.

"My mom went out at night, and she sold our sugar and food for vodka," he said through his tears. "We hid them in the basement so she wouldn't sell them."

After talking, crying, and praying together, we spooned some sugar into a plastic baggie, and Daniel solemnly placed it inside the Mad Box alongside the stick.

What his parents experienced in their own lives, I'll never know. They were born and raised in a Communist country that operated on bribes, mistrust, and corruption. Daniel and Masha's parents most likely were affected by the economic devastation following the fall of the Soviet Union. Still, it was easy to feel angry with his biological parents when I saw the pain of Daniel's grief.

Later that same day, I was baking a cake when I realized our sugar canister was empty.

"Daniel," I said as I walked from the kitchen to the living room. "Can you help me with something?"

He followed me to the kitchen and watched as I took a ten-pound bag of sugar from the pantry and opened it.

"Can you fill this for me?" I pointed to the canister and handed him the bag.

I wanted Daniel to feel the difference between this house and his old house; I wanted him to hold that difference in his hands, to picture it in his mind. In the old house, the sugar disappeared. In this house, the canister was full. I wanted him to feel it in his bones, in his body. God provided a moment of joy as I watched my new son grab that big bag of sugar and pour it into the empty canister. I prayed that his grieving soul would also be filled with sweetness.

3. CONNECT WITH ADOPTEES

Connecting with other adoptees is another way to understand your child's grief. Children who are adopted often don't understand their emotions themselves, so most of the time they aren't able to tell you what they're feeling or why. Reading what adult adoptees have to say about their experiences can shed light on what your child may be feeling.

Also try to connect your child with other kids who were adopted. Talking with someone else who may feel similar complex emotions can be helpful.

Tara Vanderwoude, a social worker and educator who was adopted, shares important insights for parents on her website, TaraVanderwoude.com: "Believing adoption is only win-win dismisses adoptees' experiences of confusion and loss and grief, shuts down conversation about the lifelong complexities that adoption brings, and impedes necessary dialogue about adoption ethics and best practices."[3]

4. SHARE YOUR CHILD'S HISTORY

Any history you have of your child's past belongs to him or her, and every detail is important. Even the smallest scrap of information can be helpful to adoptees grieving a hole in their past. One adoptee was thrilled to have a photo of himself with his birth mother, even though all that was visible of his birth mom was her elbow.

As they enter their teen years, children who have little information about their birth families may grieve in a new way as they define their identities. They may want to learn more about their past. Instead of feeling threatened, help them. Christina Romo, who was adopted at age two from South Korea, explains what many adoptees wish their parents knew: "If I ask about or search for my birth family, it doesn't mean I love you any less. I need you to know that living my life without knowledge of my birth family has been like working on a puzzle with missing pieces. Knowing about my birth family may help me feel more complete."[4]

5. MOURN TOGETHER

There may be times when all we can do is mourn with our children, because fixing their grief is impossible. Daniel longed to know what his father looked like. He had no photo, and this was a deep grief for him, especially during his teen years. Compounding this Grand Canyon–sized gap in his history was the sorrow of his only memory of his dad—the image of him hanging from a noose.

I longed to show Daniel a photo of his birth dad, to give him a history—to tell him where his father came from, what he did, what he was like—anything to dispel that one tragic portrait in Daniel's mind. But I couldn't.

I could agree with my son that his darker skin tone probably came from his father. I could say, "I bet you look just like him." But I really couldn't understand the depth of his grief, and my love for him wouldn't dispel it. Only God could offer him peace for this wound.

6. REMEMBER THE REDEEMER

As we seek to help our children grieve, we can also teach them about God the Redeemer—the One who redeems our souls from the pit (Job 33:28) and calls us by name (Isaiah 43:1), the One who redeems us from the hand of our foes (Psalm 107:2) and brings good from evil (Genesis 50:20; Romans 8:28).

We can assure our children that God is able to comfort them (2 Corinthians 1:4) and that one day they can become vessels of mercy as they use their particular losses to comfort others and be instruments of God's healing. And as they comfort others, they will also find purpose and joy.

When Daniel told me that he thought God wanted him to return to Russia to help other orphans, I let myself hope for that kind of beautiful redemption.

As your child grows and matures, you may see God work in amazing ways as He redeems a child's past and brings purpose to the pain. One couple is witnessing how God is healing their daughter Jada—and using her to help others heal as well.

"I've always told her that at the right time, in the appropriate way, God could use that suffering she went through," says adoptive mom Lisa. "That He will use it if she allows Him to use it someday."

As an older teen, Jada found herself counseling two girls as she worked at a Christian camp. Like Jada, the girls had been sexually abused, but they hadn't opened up to anyone about it before they met her. Lisa and her husband also take in foster kids when there's an emergency, and that has provided opportunities for their daughter to counsel others as well.

"We had two girls here who had been abused," Lisa recalls, "and Jada talked to them for hours. And now she's excited about stuff like that. We're starting to see fruit, because she says, 'I can reach these foster kids like no one else can.'"

As Jada has listened to others share the same thoughts she struggles with, she is gaining a new perspective on her own wounds.

"She can see that the girls weren't responsible for the abuse, that it wasn't their fault," Lisa points out. "I think that's helping her to mature. The wounded nursing the wounded is something beautiful to watch."

JOY

Helping a child grieve doesn't preclude the joys that also come with being a parent. Some may be the typical joys of parenthood that one adoptive father described this way:

> Seeing the kids wave out the window as I drive off to work, watching for me when I come home, and then running to greet me at the door. Carrying them on my shoulders. Running with them, throwing balls, sledding, and tossing them in the air. Watching them playing together with a couple of laundry baskets. Teaching them about God.

There are also special joys that come only with adoption.

Debbie Haggerty and her husband brought their girl home when she was nineteen months old. But it wasn't until 2016, when she was four, that they were finally able to adopt her.

It was quite a day for the Haggertys—especially Debbie. At bedtime her daughter told her, "When I was a baby, I stole your heart. Because babies don't have hearts. But now I have a heart, because I have yours."

Precious words such as these are the joyful notes in the song of adoption. This song might burst full throated into your life through a school assignment, an unexpected hug, or a child's simple prayer ("Thank You, God, for my family").

One day less than a year after Jeff and I adopted Daniel and Masha, Masha brought home a Mother's Day present for me—a decorated paper titled "What I Remember about My Mother," which I now have framed. Here's what it says:

> Mom, I remember when you adopted me. I remember when you drove us to the school. I remember my first day I met you, you loved me right away. I remember when we made cookies together. I remember when I went to the dentist and it was my first time, then you sat with me.

These sweetly arranged notes can arrive in as many ways as an infinite God can devise. I'm blessed to have a video of our arrival at the orphanage in Russia, when Masha came running to me with excitement after our five months of separation, yelling "Mommy, Mommy" in Russian and giving me a big hug.

"There have been so many joys," says Jake Warren, despite the difficulties involved in adopting a blind child from a Bulgarian orphanage.

"Before my daughter could fully grasp the English language, I would still pray with her in English," Jake recalls. "I would say the prayer with her, and she would repeat and repeat it. The day she asked me if she could pray was a proud moment, to say the least. That first time they ask to pray, or that first 'I love you'— those are the things you can't put a price tag on."

HARD-WON JOY

There are also hard-won joys as you see your child with a traumatic past overcome physical, emotional, spiritual, or academic obstacles.

One adoptive mom experienced a deeply joyful moment that was five years in the making. Kelly and her husband, Jon, adopted Ryan when he was a toddler.

"When he was little, he would only go to other women, and he would scream when I touched him," Kelly says. "That was horrible. It was like he knew that I was the one disrupting his life."

Ryan had a severe attachment disorder. To develop a special attachment with him, Kelly and Jon asked people not to put Ryan on their laps or pick him up, but those requests were ignored.

"He'd go to every woman constantly instead of me," Kelly remembers. "He never let me hold him; he would always struggle to get away. When I hugged him, it was always with the feeling that he didn't really care, that he didn't like it."

Even after five years, Kelly felt as if her son had never bonded with her. And then something happened one day as she was about to leave for a weekend getaway with friends. After preparing her family for her absence, Kelly was ready and waiting for her ride when seven-year-old Ryan noticed his mother standing at the door with her bags.

Suddenly he realized she was leaving.

"I had told him already, but you know how kids don't always listen. It just hit him. He was probably thinking, *Hey, wait a minute! Mom's going somewhere.*"

"Where you going?" Ryan asked in his little-boy voice.

"I'm going scrapbooking," Kelly said. "But I'll be back home tomorrow night."

And then something strange happened: Ryan began to cry.

"When will you be back?" he asked through his tears.

It was then—for the first time after five years of caring for this boy—that Kelly thought, *He loves me!*

"It was an amazing moment—the moment of my life," Kelly reflects. "It was the first time Ryan actually missed me. That's such a small moment; most people would say, 'Oh, big deal.'" But for Kelly, it was a tender, sweet victory. "Definitely a 'worth it' moment."

When Ryan was ten, Kelly had to leave on a long trip. "Ryan

was the only one of my children who cried when I left. He even cried at the airport. That touched me too. He didn't usually do that kind of stuff. But he did it twice. Now I know Ryan loves me."

FRUITFUL JOY

Perhaps the best joy is knowing that your child believes in Jesus.

It had been a day like most in 2004 after I had instantly become a mother of four instead of two—a day filled with hugging, helping, cooking, cleaning, and teaching my new kids everything from Bible stories and the names of emotions to how to use a toaster. On any given night, I might spend two hours encouraging Daniel while trying to convince him that he could do his math homework (and he could). But that night I was so exhausted that my only prayer before dropping into bed was *Help me. Give me a word. Let me hear from You.*

The next morning, Masha managed with her limited English to tell me about her dreams. In the first dream, God was building a house for us. The second dream was about God and me.

"You were outside digging in the dirt, planting seeds," Masha told me as she pointed out the kitchen window. "Then you asked God to take the seeds and make them into trees with very big apples that weren't sour. And then God did it."

This tiny girl loved apples; she ate them so quickly—core and all—that I had to ration them. So the thought of big, sweet apples pleased her. She had no idea that she was delivering an encouraging message from God to me.

I know this is hard work, and you're tired, God whispered, *but you're planting good seed that will become good fruit.*

One day about two weeks later, Daniel became especially oppositional, trying to find any opportunity to argue and fight with me. He ended the day screaming and crying. That night as we prayed, my husband asked God to work a miracle in Daniel's heart.

The next day was a Sunday, and at that time Jeff and my other kids went to Sunday school while Daniel, Masha, and I had our own Sunday school at home. At breakfast, Masha told me about another dream.

"Me and Daniel were going to these big apple trees in our yard, and they had beautiful, big apples."

"Uh-huh," I mumbled as I dished out eggs to my Russian kids who hated cereal.

"But some of the apples were already picked. That's because you picked the apples, Mom. You brought them into the house."

I listened distractedly as I fed them breakfast and gathered items for our Sunday school lesson. After I read a Bible story to Masha and Daniel and we did a craft about kids praying, Daniel started asking questions about prayer.

"I don't know how to pray," he said.

"Praying is like talking to God," I told him. Then I explained how he and Masha could have Jesus with them all the time, and they could pray and talk to Him whenever they wanted. But first they had to decide to believe in Jesus. If they believed in Jesus, they would go to heaven when they died. So they both prayed a simple prayer that I modeled, which was probably something like this: "Jesus, I believe in You. I'm sorry for the bad things I've done. Thank You for loving me. Come into my heart and help me be like You."

Wondering if the prayers were valid—after all, they were just learning English and about God—I herded the kids into the car and drove to church to meet the rest of the family. As I drove, I suddenly remembered Masha's dream about how I had gathered the apples and brought them into the house. And then I heard the Lord assuring me that the transaction was the real deal.

You brought spiritual fruit into My house this morning, He whispered. I knew then that my two youngest kids had entered His kingdom, and all of heaven was rejoicing along with me.

Look forward to the joy of loving your children: blowing bubbles while you all laugh, building snowmen, praying and singing with them, and cuddling on the couch. Just know that you may also need to grieve with them. Being aware of this possibility will help you understand their behaviors and what they need from you.

✏ *Rest Stop*

What might your child need to grieve? How might she or he show that grief? Ask God to help you recognize and respond to your child's grief. Record your thoughts about this and answers to prayer on the journal page. At the same time, start a joy record of good times with your child. This could be as easy as taking photos and then sending them to an online service that prints them in a book and delivers it directly to your home.

My Journey to Adoption

DATE _____

For everything there is a season, and a time for every
matter under heaven: . . . a time to weep, and a time
to laugh; a time to mourn, and a time to dance.

Ecclesiastes 3:1, 4

CHAPTER 12

A Deeper Trust

It is easy to say you believe a rope to be strong and sound as long as you are merely using it to cord a box. But suppose you had to hang by that rope over a precipice. Wouldn't you then first discover how much you really trusted it?

C. S. LEWIS
A Grief Observed

It was a sunny, mild September day in Wisconsin, and I was exhausted. My four children were still in school, and I had some time before mom duty started again.

Three months earlier, we'd brought our two preteens home from Russia to join our thirteen- and fourteen-year-old birth kids. Instantly I was cooking for six and caring for four kids while also writing freelance newspaper articles to help pay the bills.

Daniel and Masha spoke little English, so communicating required large quantities of time and energy. Added to the long list of typical mom jobs, I was also "Mom the English teacher," "Mom the therapist," and "Mom the Sunday school teacher." My new children were emotionally needy, to say the least, and constantly sought my hugs and affection. Their love tanks were on empty, and every time they came near me, they were basically crying, "Fill 'er up!" At one point, I desperately wanted a day alone so no one would touch me!

In addition to this physical and emotional weariness, I was also worried. Our financial situation was bleak, and the sale of a business had fallen through. We'd been counting on that sale.

On this particular fall day, I used those few moments I had before becoming "Mom the school bus" to walk down to our dock and dangle my feet in the lake water. As I stepped onto the weathered wooden boards, I prayed, *Lord, help me. Help me trust You more.*

I was about to sit down when I noticed a large spiderweb attached to one of the dock's poles. As I watched the web swaying in the light breeze, I noticed how fragile it seemed, yet how it moved in the wind without breaking. The narrow end of the spiderweb was attached to a small boat anchor left sitting on the dock.

Trust Me, God told my spirit in that moment. *You may feel as fragile as this spiderweb looks, but you are anchored to Me. Don't forget that. The wind may blow, but I'm here.*

A SACRIFICIAL ELEMENT

It turns out that being compared to a spiderweb is a good thing. By weight, spider silk is as strong as steel. Spider silk and webs are so resilient that scientists say researching them could affect engineering, medicine, and computer networks in a big way. A key property of spider silk that helps make webs so strong "is something previously considered a weakness: the way it can stretch and soften at first when pulled, and then stiffen again as the force of the pulling increases."[1]

If you're feeling stretched and blown by the wind during the adoption process or as you care for your new child, think of yourself as a spiderweb. And remember the apostle Paul's words: "When I am weak, then I am strong" (2 Corinthians 12:10).

The stretching induced by the challenges and the softening brought on by multiple emotions are actually part of your strength as you lean into God. With Him as your anchor, you'll have what you need to "stiffen" like spider silk when stronger hurricane forces blow.

MIT studies show that spiderwebs can be bashed about quite a bit without failing. Even if the web is damaged in one spot, it doesn't mean it's useless. The broken part is considered localized damage, and it often doesn't even need to be repaired. Scientists call this the web's *sacrificial element*—an area that can be injured without causing mechanical failure of the overall structure.[2]

When you feel damaged, label the injury your sacrificial element. It won't destroy you. Adjusting to the needs of your new child and helping him or her feel safe in your home can be difficult, but God "gives power and strength to his people" (Psalm 68:35). You are stronger than you think when you choose to keep trusting in the Lord.

AFTER THE HONEYMOON PERIOD

I experienced my own sacrificial element during the first year with our new son. After three months of a honeymoon period (when Daniel was on his best behavior with us), he began feeling safe enough to share his pain. As psychologists will tell you, children speak volumes though their behavior.

In my house, that meant Daniel would try to anger me from the moment I stepped out of my bedroom to the moment he went to sleep. Unconsciously, he wanted my feelings to reflect his inner turmoil; he wanted to share the anxiety, anger, shame, and hopelessness he'd been storing up for twelve years. This was his method of communicating the anger he felt toward his birth mom for abandoning him. He wanted me to feel like he did.

Psychologists call this *inducement*, and let me tell you, it works! I had no idea what was happening in my home until my friend—also an adoptive mother—gave me a cassette tape of a seminar session on this topic.

Maris Blechner, a licensed clinical social worker and the executive director of an adoption service in New York, writes,

> Those of us who live or work with adopted children need to understand that inducement is absolutely the language of the abandoned. . . .
>
> Abandoned children are experts at setting up a situation to make someone special feel exactly how that child feels. . . .
>
> As we have learned directly from adoptees, the sense of having been abandoned is central to adoptees' experience. . . .
>
> How does an abandoned person feel? Isolated, guilty, lost, filled with profound sorrow, enraged, worthless, hopeless, helpless, and most of all, crazy. . . .
>
> It is only when a child believes that he is finally going to be adopted, and will finally have a real family, that the inducement begins.[3]

Inducement is actually a sign that a child is beginning to trust you, and yet it doesn't feel remotely like that. After four months, I was experiencing many of the emotions Daniel wanted to share with me—rage, shame, guilt, and hopelessness.

Our new son was too terrified to trust us, because the last time he'd trusted parents, they had both deserted him. And that had been devastating. He wanted and needed intimacy, yet he feared it at the same time. He would let me come close to him, only to push me away. He would often say, "You're not my real mom. You're not the boss of me. You're not the king of me!"

It's easy to understand that a child is afraid to get too close to his new mother, to risk being abandoned and deeply hurt once more. What is *not* so easy is living with the behaviors springing from these emotions.

LIVING WITHOUT TRUST

Daniel watched my every move, word, and facial expression (the psychological label for this is *hypervigilance*). He was terrified that we would send him back to Russia, even though we repeatedly told him we would never do that, that he was our son forever, and that we loved him very much.

When I was on the telephone, Daniel would listen intently and then yell at me afterward, saying, "You're planning to meet a man! You're going to leave!" He was afraid I would become his birth mom, the one who left him alone so she could be with men. If I went into another room, he would ask me where I was going. He was highly anxious, negative, and oppositional for the first year he was with us, and living with someone who has those traits is extremely stressful.

> **TIPS FOR BUILDING TRUST**
>
> - *Give repetitive reassurance.* Tell your child again and again that you will never leave, that you will always be his or her parents. It's especially important to say this when your child makes a mistake or needs to be corrected.
> - *Make up for missed bonding.* Find ways to increase physical touch and eye contact. Rock your child, wash your child's hair, put on skin lotion, play Twister, have staring contests to increase bonding eye contact, snuggle while watching TV or reading a book, paint fingernails, or put on false tattoos.
> - *Stick to a regular schedule.* Follow regular bedtime and mealtime routines to build a sense of security.
> - *Talk about the future.* Discuss plans for your child's next birthday, what you'll do together next summer, or what your child wants to be when he or she grows up.[4]

I often reassured Daniel that I wasn't like his Russian mother. One day he replied, "But people can change."

That stopped me in my tracks. He was right. People *can* change. Daniel was a smart boy with a sensitive heart. I loved him, but he was driving me crazy! He expected the worst. If I cheerfully came home from grocery shopping saying, "I bought ice cream!" he would say, "I bet it's cherry or banana ice cream. Because I hate cherry and banana." We were living with his Debbie Downer heart, which had been hurt so many times that he anticipated the worst.

We learned to empty our mailbox before Daniel did, because he would imagine the letters were part of our plan to return him to Russia. If he found a health insurance statement in the mail with his name on it, hours of emotional upheaval would follow.

During a church sermon, he would tap me with his bulletin and say, "Do you not like me for doing that?" He knew I didn't like the tapping. But even as he feared becoming too close to me, he also had a voracious need for my attention. He would resort to complaining on a daily basis about a hurting body part just so I would focus on him.

At some point, I realized he was displaying separation anxiety—just as a toddler would—in addition to his ever-present fear of abandonment. Preparing Daniel for the schedule of the day was important. We also prepared him for our once-a-week "special time for Mom and Dad."

Daniel didn't like special time for Mom and Dad. One Friday morning after reminding him that Jeff and I would be dining out that evening, I drove Daniel to school. As I pulled into the parking lot, he asked in a cheery voice, "Mom, can I tell you something?"

"Of course, honey," I said, thrilled that he wanted to talk.

"I'm going to wreck your whole day. You are a bad mom. You're a really bad mom."

Then he opened the door and stepped out of the van. Smiling at me, he shut the door, waved good-bye, and sauntered down the sidewalk to the school's entrance.

That day I thought he was trying to punish me for our "special time" that didn't include him. No matter what Jeff and I did, he felt rejected. And this process of inducement, which sometimes felt like mind games to me, was emotionally draining.

If you experience inducement, knowing that your child might be "sharing" his or her emotions with you in this way can keep you sane and help you realize this is a step toward trusting you.

A LOSE-LOSE SITUATION

Once after bedtime prayers, Daniel asked what I would think if he called me "Mrs. Holmquist." I said I wouldn't like it at all because I was his mom.

"Okay," he said. "Good night, Mrs. Holmquist." And he then called me Mrs. Holmquist for days, knowing it annoyed me.

If I ignored him and didn't react to his provocation, he would say, "See, Mrs. Holmquist, you're not my mom. You said if I called you Mrs. Holmquist, it would make you feel bad, but it doesn't, so you don't love me."

He would become angry if I hugged him only once instead of twice or moved his backpack out of the way, because to him that meant I didn't love him. He would sabotage a pleasant outing by being negative and oppositional.

Another day, after I'd spent time swimming with him in our lake, I told him I was tired and was going to sit on our dock and read a book. Because he wanted me to keep swimming with him, he was furious and started screaming, "You're reading a book about naked people!" I tried to calm him by telling him what I was reading, but he continued to scream from the lake. I eventually closed my book and went inside.

When he came inside to apologize and saw that I was talking on the phone, his anxiety returned, and he yelled, "You're a liar! You're not reading a book! You're on the phone!"

An offhand conversation would often lead to an angry outburst. One day my daughter Anna told me about a nineteen-year-old girl who had been married twice. Daniel took that statement and transformed it into this: "Mom, you've been married before! And you kept it a secret!"

Another time, as we were driving home from a therapy appointment, Daniel tried jumping out of the car as it sped sixty miles per hour down a freeway. Since my husband was at the wheel, I had to jump into the backseat, lock my legs around Daniel, and pull him away from the door.

SHAME AND GUILT

I didn't always respond to these behaviors and other seemingly crazy ones in a rational, calm way. So in addition to the stress and difficulty of trying to understand Daniel's behaviors and help him heal, I was also filled with shame and guilt for the times I lost my temper with him and sounded and acted like a child myself—not an adult, and definitely not a Christian woman. One day I was determined not to respond to his attempts to anger me.

"You are not going to make me mad," I told him, which wasn't a wise move on my part. That only made him redouble his efforts.

I managed to stay calm and cool for more than two days in the face of Daniel's provocations. And then, finally, I blew my top. My fifteen-year-old daughter actually told me to go to my room!

"See," Daniel said. "I made you mad!"

It was a way he could exert control. He wasn't in control when his father and mother disappeared, or when he was yanked from his home and placed in an orphanage, or when he never saw his grandparents again. He wasn't in control when the big kids beat him at the orphanage. Now he was determined to be the one in charge and stay safe!

A HOPELESS NIGHT

I tell you these stories so you have some sense of the hopelessness I was feeling one night about seven months after we had brought Daniel home. I felt like a failure in so many ways, even though I was trying to do everything the therapists and books suggested.

I had read a tower of books about adoption and raising children who had been traumatized. I had tried to implement anything and everything I could to help my son. We had been through two therapists. Jeff and I had prayed for him, with him, and over him. We weren't sure what else to do. I was beginning to think this boy would never trust me, and we would have to live with his trauma forever. I couldn't imagine life continuing this way, with this level of daily stress.

After one especially difficult and shame-inducing day with Daniel, a day when I'd lost complete control of my emotions, I began to doubt God's very existence.

Where are You, God?!

I'd lost my temper with my son, and now I was angry with God, too.

Why aren't You healing Daniel? I thought. *Are You even there?*

As I retreated to my bedroom in complete despair, my husband came in with my Bible in his hand.

"Read this," Jeff said as he tossed the Bible on our bed. He was smart enough to know I needed God's intervention at this point, not his.

"Why should I?" I countered. "It won't make any difference!" (This from a woman who loved God's Word and had painted Bible verses on the walls of her house!)

Jeff left the room, and eventually I flipped open the Bible. It just happened to land at Lamentations 3. (What are the odds of a Bible's falling open to a page in this five-chapter book?)

I began reading these words:

> He has broken my teeth with gravel;
> > he has trampled me in the dust.
> I have been deprived of peace;
> > I have forgotten what prosperity is.
> So I say, "My splendor is gone
> > and all that I had hoped from the LORD."
>
> 3:16-18, NIV

As I read this passage from Lamentations, I sensed God's presence. *Yes, Lord*, I thought. *I feel trampled and broken!*

I read on:

> I remember my affliction and my wandering,
> > the bitterness and the gall.
> I well remember them,
> > and my soul is downcast within me.
>
> 3:19-20, NIV

In my spirit, I felt God saying, *I know how you feel, Julie.*

Knowing He understood my feelings was comforting. I realized that He was still with me, even though my faith in Him had almost disappeared.

Then I read verses 21-25:

> Yet this I call to mind
> > And therefore I have hope:

Because of the LORD's great love we are not consumed,
for his compassions never fail.
They are new every morning;
great is your faithfulness.
I say to myself, "The LORD is my portion;
therefore I will wait for him."

The LORD is good to those *whose hope is in him.*
NIV, EMPHASIS ADDED

The Lord let me know that I had hoped in therapists, in books, in techniques—but when all seemed lost, they really weren't the source of hope. I was to *hope in Him alone.* I had forgotten the strength of God's promises—my anchor, as Hebrews 6:19 says: "We have this hope as an anchor for the soul, firm and secure" (NIV).

Matthew Henry described our hope this way:

We are in this world as a ship at sea, liable to be tossed
up and down, and in danger of being cast away. . . . We
have need of an anchor to keep us sure and steady. . . .
Gospel hope is our anchor . . . in our stormy passage
through this world. . . . It is sure and stedfast, or else
it could not keep us so. . . . The free grace of God,
the merits and mediation of Christ, and the powerful
influences of his Spirit, are the grounds of his hope, and
so it is a stedfast hope. Jesus Christ is the object and
ground of the believer's hope.[5]

HOPE IN GOD

As I read Lamentations that evening, the Lord showed me that I needed to trust Him and hope in Him in a deeper way, just as Daniel needed to learn to trust me. I was learning the same lesson as my new son!

That night, my trust was so small, I'd almost denied God's existence. My despair pushed me to ask, "Should I trust God or abandon Him?" This was basically the same question Daniel was asking himself about me: *Should I trust this new mom? Or will she hurt me the way the other one did? Should I reject her?* Many children may feel like this when they're adopted.

Trust is such a basic yet vital requirement of healthy relationships. We don't realize how important it is until it's not there.

Ernie Johnson Jr. and his wife, Cheryl, adopted two preteen girls who had lived in half a dozen foster homes.

"I would tell my friends that the girls didn't have many possessions, but they had a lot of baggage," Ernie writes in his book *Unscripted*. "Unpacking it was difficult. We were trying to show them love. They were trying to trust that we were not going to be just another stop on the road."[6]

Early on, Cheryl and her new daughter Allison had this conversation:

> "Allison, you have to realize that this is it. This is your forever home."
>
> "I have a question."
>
> "Go ahead, hon."
>
> "How long will forever be this time?"[7]

When our children don't trust us, it can be maddening. You may think as I did, *Doesn't this kid see how much I love him? Doesn't he know that God chose him for us, that we traveled halfway around the world for him? Doesn't he remember that I provide for his every need, that I make his every meal? Has he forgotten that I pray for him and read to him? I take him to the doctor, help him with his homework, cry and laugh with him. I've been the same faithful mom day after day, month after month for more than a year now . . . but he still doesn't trust me!*

Don't we often act this way with the Lord? He may have provided for us for years, but a crisis hits, and our faith begins to waver. That's what happened to me that evening. As I sat on my bed doubting God's existence, perhaps He was thinking, *Doesn't this child see how much I love her? Doesn't she know that I died for her, that I chose her before time began? Doesn't she remember that I've provided for all of her needs for years and years? Has she forgotten that I've always been there to comfort her and calm her fears? Doesn't she realize that I listen to every one of her prayers? I have been the same faithful God to her day after day, year after year . . . and yet she doesn't trust Me with this situation!*

It was no coincidence that God's many lessons for me paralleled what Daniel needed to learn. Because of this, I developed a deep empathy for Daniel's struggles, and he saw he wasn't alone. Time after time, Daniel saw me ask forgiveness, push aside negativity and the lies of Satan, and choose to trust God, whose mercies are new every morning—for Daniel and for me. Time after time, Daniel would ask for forgiveness. Once he apologized by making me a paper box with a heart inside shaped from a pink pipe cleaner.

And then we would start again. I purchased a plaque that said "Every day is a new beginning" and hung it in our kitchen. As we stumbled about trying to love each other—sometimes failing and sometimes succeeding—Daniel and I drew strength from God's new mercies and new beginnings.

One of the many names of God is "Miqweh Yisrael"—"Hope of Israel." Ann Spangler writes in *Praying the Names of God,*

Hope is the great stabilizer. It steadies us in times of fear and difficulty, not because we know that everything will turn out as we want, but because we know that God is trustworthy. . . . Biblical hope finds its roots in God and

in his goodness, mercy, and power. We exercise our hope
when we endure patiently. We nurture our hope when
we read God's Word.[8]

Because of that night more than a decade ago, I have never
again doubted His existence no matter how painful the circumstances have been (and make no mistake, more painful circumstances did arrive). In my despair, God gave me His hope through
His Word, and it was enough.

His hope is enough for you, too. God is aware of your circumstances, your challenges, your doubts and fears. If you find your
trust beginning to crumble as you deal with your child's behaviors or other challenges, flip open your Bible, God's living Word.
Listen to the Hope of Israel! Let Him teach you a deeper trust.
He says to you, *Hope in Me alone!*

✏ *Rest Stop*

Is your trust in God weakening because of weariness or crisis?
Meditate on Job 13:15, Psalm 33:18, Psalm 130:6-7, and Isaiah
40:31. Ask God to renew your hope in Him and help you trust
Him no matter the circumstances. Record your thoughts on your
journal page.

My Journey to Adoption

DATE _____

Trust in him at all times, O people; pour out your
heart before him; God is a refuge for us.

Psalm 62:8

CHAPTER 13

Spiritual Battles

*I'm not afraid of the devil. . . . He can't handle the One to whom
I'm joined; he can't handle the One to whom I'm united; he
can't handle the One whose nature dwells in my nature.*

A. W. TOZER

pastor

Your daughter swears at you and says she wants to live with her *real* mother. Your son bangs his head into the wall, and your wife blames you for upsetting him. You wake up one morning and find yourself wanting to jump in the car and never come home. Raising a child with a tough beginning can be challenging, and Satan is happy to use those challenges to break the unity of your family. That's why you'll need to be alert.

If you adopt a child who has been neglected, abused, and unloved, the Evil One wants to use what he's already begun: He wants the destruction of that child's family to continue and flow into yours. Satan certainly doesn't want a family to model the gospel and "religion that is pure and undefiled" before God (James 1:27).

According to Project 1.27 president and adoptive mom Shelly Radic, adoptive parents *will* experience spiritual opposition as they love their children and seek their healing.[1]

Let me emphasize that it's important to understand your child and any trauma he or she may have faced and to make use of therapies and trauma-informed parenting strategies if needed. Your child may have complex medical and therapeutic issues that require professional help. Don't make the mistake of ignoring highly skilled people God has provided to aid your child.

But as you seek professional help and God's wisdom, it's also wise to consider the unseen realm of the Enemy and his schemes to ruin your family. After all, the apostle Paul clearly stated that we do have opposition: "Our struggle is not against flesh and blood, but against the rulers, against the authorities, against the powers of this dark world and against the spiritual forces of evil in the heavenly realms" (Ephesians 6:12, NIV). And 1 Peter 5:8 tells us to "be alert and of sober mind. Your enemy the devil prowls around like a roaring lion looking for someone to devour" (NIV).

I've read that lions don't roar when they attack their prey. They are quiet as they look for stragglers—the weak animals far behind the pack, the isolated ones. Most likely your child has come to you in a weakened, hurt state. It's also easy for hurt children to think they're alone—that no one else has experienced what they have. You also may feel isolated if you experience stress and struggle with your new child, especially if you have no one around you who understands adoption issues. If you have bio-logical children, they may be feeling neglected and lonely as you spend more time with your new child.

Satan will try to use those situations, but he will do so quietly. That's why it's important to be aware of potential spiritual battles as you begin your adoption journey. Because Jesus Christ won the ultimate victory over Satan when He died on the cross (Colossians 2:14-15), there's nothing to fear. One day God will send the Devil to "the lake of burning sulfur" (Revelation 20:10, NIV), but right now he remains a shrewd adversary.

"Satan does not believe in the sanctity of life, the sanctity of marriage, or the beauty of the family," writes Pastor Brian Borgman, an adoptive father and the author of *After They Are Yours: The Grace and Grit of Adoption.* "He will use your adoptive struggles to wage war on your marriage, on your family, and on your faith."[2]

ASK "WHY?"

Children who've experienced past trauma and loss can be extra vulnerable to Satan's lies. They may doubt their new parents' love, feel less important than biological siblings, expect rejection, and decide they are inherently "bad" because their biological family didn't keep them. They may be thinking, *This isn't my real family. No one loves me. I can't trust anyone. I'm stupid. I'm no good.*

Mary DeMuth grew up in a home full of drug abuse and was sexually abused at age five. She ended up being cared for by grandparents who conveyed a message that caring for Mary was an inconvenience. In her book *Beautiful Battle: A Woman's Guide to Spiritual Warfare*, DeMuth writes about the consequent "gaping mother and father hole" in her life and how she has battled the lies Satan whispered about her. "Our raw woundedness is the primary opening the enemy uses to attack our souls," she observes.[3]

Satan can use to his advantage the messages abandoned and abused children acquire, such as "You're insignificant. You deserve this pain. No one will want you!"

Brian and Ariel Borgman learned this the hard way after adopting a neglected toddler who was eventually diagnosed with fetal alcohol spectrum disorder and attention deficit hyperactivity disorder. It wasn't until their son, Alex, was twelve that his parents understood why he was often so oppositional toward his adoptive mother.

One evening Alex tearfully asked his mother why his birth

mom didn't want him. As the Borgmans talked with their son, Brian asked this question: "Alex, I know you and your mom have always butted heads and struggled with each other. Do you know why?" His son replied, "I thought that Mom might not want me either."[4]

This boy's idea that his adoptive mom didn't really want him was obviously a lie that Satan didn't want exposed.

If your child seems disrespectful and oppositional, pay special attention to adoption issues that may be at the root of the behavior: loss, rejection, grief, guilt, shame, intimacy, control, and identity. And don't hesitate to seek professional help to better understand how the past has affected your child. Ask God to help you uncover the lies of Satan that are operating in your child's mind, and then help your child learn God's truth for every lie you uncover together.

AVOID OFFENSE

Pray that God will point out when pride is in control so you can avoid being offended by your child's behavior. The goal is to sidestep resentment so you can focus on understanding your child's actions and looking for ways to meet underlying needs or find better ways to handle problems.

It's easy to be offended if our children defy us, ignore us, or say hurtful things to our faces. We're only human. But other factors, such as a brain affected by trauma, may be influencing a child's behavior. For instance, let's say a parent continually tells a child to do three chores, and she does only one. It could be that she simply can't retain all three chores in her mind. Or if your child won't answer you and shuts down, she may be feeling unsafe and threatened because of painful events from the past.

Unfortunately, Satan counts on our feeling hurt and prideful. I'm sure he loves to hear parents say, "No child of *mine* is going to talk to *me* that way!" Once we say that, we're acting in pride and thinking of ourselves instead of the child. During that first challenging year with Daniel, there were too many times when I took offense at his responses without considering why he said what he did. I fell for the subtle temptation of the Evil One to take offense, and that created chaos in our home.

As Pastor John Bevere writes, "Often when we are offended we see ourselves as victims and blame those who have hurt us."[5] If you feel offended by your child, tell yourself you're not the victim—you're the adult. Ask God to help you see the situation with His eyes of love and discernment. Make this declaration to the Lord, as Bevere recommends: "Reveal my heart's true condition, and do not allow hidden offense to clothe me with pride."[6]

RECOGNIZE SATAN'S LIES

We faced a spiritual battle not long after Daniel accepted Christ when he was twelve. Jeff and I were playing a game with Daniel in the living room when all of a sudden, our son's expression turned grim.

"What's wrong, Daniel?" I asked.

"I don't have Jesus in my heart," he said in a despairing tone. "Someone else is in my heart."

"Why do you say that?"

"Because I had bad thoughts about you and Dad."

Since my son had just crossed from the kingdom of darkness into the kingdom of light, the source of Daniel's thoughts seemed apparent to me. I told him Jesus did indeed live in his heart, and because of that, Satan wasn't happy. The father of lies was trying to fool him.

"Tell Satan that he is a liar," I explained. "Tell him to go away because you belong to Jesus now."

Daniel considered what I said as he went to take a shower. That's where he resisted Satan (James 4:7). When Daniel stepped out of the bathroom, a look of peace flooded his face, and tears of joy streamed down his cheeks. He was greatly relieved.

On that occasion, I helped my son identify the lies of Satan and taught him to respond to the Devil's deception. Unfortunately, I didn't always identify the Enemy when I should have.

Early on, Daniel would often accuse me of loving my biological children more than him, and I would then reaffirm my "forever" love for him. But I wish I had also reminded him that his siblings and I were not the enemy. I could have told him that Satan wanted to stir up jealousy in his heart, because the Enemy looks for ways to divide a family. We could have discussed ways to resist Satan and, together, put on the belt of truth.

If Satan's lies have already invaded a child's mind because of adoption—*I'm not worth anything because my real parents didn't want me*—the battle plan in Ephesians 6:13-18 is a lifeline.

Satan can also attack parents as we find ourselves responding to difficult situations in sinful ways. Satan will use our weaknesses to tempt us to keep sinning. He's happy when he sees us stuck in a cycle of sin and guilt. That's when he'll tell us we're failures as Christians and parents, hoping we won't remember that God has equipped us through His Word (2 Timothy 3:16-17), and we're "joint heirs" with Christ (Romans 8:16-17, NKJV).

In Luke 22:31, Jesus says to Peter, "Simon, Simon, Satan has asked to sift all of you as wheat" (NIV). To sift wheat, people used a *flail*—a threshing device made of sticks. They would repeatedly beat the wheat with the flail so the heads of grain would separate from the chaff. To sift you, Satan will attempt to beat you down with his lies and then tempt you in a way that will push you away from God. Look at the same statement in *The Message*: "Simon, stay on your toes. Satan has tried his best to separate all of you from me, like chaff from wheat."

Following are four messages the Evil One likes to tell adoptive parents who are struggling. Don't believe them!

1. GIVE UP

One woman wanted to stop the adoption process after she discovered that the young girl she and her husband planned to adopt had been sexually abused. Michelle and Eric had adopted other children, and Michelle knew enough to anticipate a long, difficult road ahead to help this wounded child heal.

"Right away, Satan was attacking me. I wrestled and wrestled with that, thinking, *I can't take this child home. I don't have the faintest idea what to do about this kind of issue.* I knew how selfish I was. And I thought, *Why would God pick me to do this? Why would He pick someone so selfish?*"

After successfully battling Satan's lies, Michelle remained true to the couple's decision to adopt the girl. She and her husband have spent years teaching their daughter about God and helping her heal. Now older, this former orphan has counseled other kids who have been abused.

2. ESCAPE

During the difficult first year with Daniel in our home, I had times when I didn't want to return to my house and deal with conflict and struggle. One day as I was driving home, an idea popped into my head to avoid my house and instead drown my sorrows in alcohol. On that day, in that moment, I knew Satan was tempting me. He knew my weaknesses; he knew that if I started leaning on alcohol for comfort and to avoid reality, it would have a destructive effect on my entire family—especially on Daniel, who had already witnessed an alcoholic mother and was terrified I would become just like her. Satan would have loved for me to become dependent on alcohol.

The Evil One is most happy when he is urging us to escape from the adversity of life in a way that's unhealthy and separates us from Jesus. And he'll tailor his temptation to your weaknesses. What tempted me probably isn't what would tempt you.

That day in the car, I resisted Satan (James 4:7), took "every thought captive to obey Christ" (2 Corinthians 10:5), and drove home.

I've found that when I'm stretched emotionally and physically, I'm most vulnerable to Satan's attacks. That's why rest is so important. Do your best to plan healthy and regular respites so you can avoid the Evil One's prompts to escape in a way that's destructive for you and your family.

3. BLAME YOUR CHILD OR SPOUSE

If you deal with struggles for an extended period of time, Satan may try to convince you that your spouse and your child are the enemies when he is the one you need to battle.

Brian Borgman recalls a stressful time when he fell into this trap after he and his wife didn't respond well to one of their son's angry eruptions:

> There was a growing tension between the two of us. Ariel told me how angry and hurt she was, and then I said it.
>
> "This is your fault. You wanted to adopt him. If you had only listened to me! I told you he would bring turmoil into our family."
>
> I still can't believe I said it.
>
> The words hurt her so badly. . . . My flesh was at work—my selfish, sinful, wicked heart. But Satan was also at work. We had given him a foothold and he was on the

attack. After a while, we realized what was happening. I asked for forgiveness. We reconciled and prayed. I knew I had lost my warfare mentality, and it had cost us.[7]

One adoptive mother I know quickly begins to pray when her daughter starts pushing her buttons. She stops everything and drops to her knees. Eventually the girl calms down. This mom has learned that her daughter isn't the adversary—Satan is.

4. STOP BELIEVING

Right before Jeff and I adopted our kids, I was suddenly surrounded by Bible studies and sermons on the book of Job. I sensed the Holy Spirit warning me that I would deal with painful difficulties after the adoption. While I recognized Job's pain from losing everything he had, including his health, I failed to consider an obvious point: He was fighting a spiritual battle as Satan tried to make him turn away from God. Yet Job didn't deny "the words of the Holy One" (Job 6:10). Instead, he said, "Though he slay me, I will hope in him" (13:15). He actually became more intimate with God through the experience.

Looking back, I now see that the ongoing, intense struggles in our home prompted me to doubt God's existence, and I began listening to Satan's lies: *He's not healing Daniel, so God isn't here. He's not real. Everything you thought was true was a figment of your imagination. What has He done to help you?* It was by God's grace that I heard His offer of hope in Lamentations 3:21-25. Now I can say, like Job, that I have a stronger faith and am closer to God because of that trial.

REBUILD THE WALL

When Nehemiah brought the exiled Jews back to Jerusalem to rebuild the city's walls that lay in rubble and ashes, they had to work hard. Yes, God was on their side, but they faced strong opposition. Their enemies made it clear that these rebuilders were a threat, and they wanted them dead. So Nehemiah and God's people took turns guarding the rebuilt sections of the wall while they continued to work.

As you work to love and build up a child who may be wounded, make sure you also guard against the opposition. Listen to the message Nehemiah gave God's people: "I looked and arose and said to the nobles and to the officials and to the rest of the people, 'Do not be afraid of [the enemy]. Remember the Lord, who is great and awesome, and fight for your brothers, your sons, your daughters, your wives, and your homes'" (Nehemiah 4:14).

Never forget that almighty God has given you powerful weapons so you can keep your family unified and close to Him. Let's consider a few of those weapons in the next chapter.

✒ Rest Stop

What do you believe about Satan? Does it match what Scripture says about him? Consider these verses as you pray and journal:

> [Jesus] said to [His disciples], "I saw Satan fall like lightning from heaven. Behold, I have given you authority to tread on serpents and scorpions, and over all the power of the enemy, and nothing shall hurt you."
> LUKE 10:17-19

> When [the devil] lies, he speaks out of his own character, for he is a liar and the father of lies.
> JOHN 8:44

> Submit yourselves therefore to God. Resist the devil, and he will flee from you.
> JAMES 4:7

My Journey to Adoption

DATE_____

There is no neutral ground in the universe: every
square inch, every split second, is claimed by
God and counterclaimed by Satan.

C. S. Lewis, *Christian Reflections*

CHAPTER 14

Spiritual Weapons

*Faith, without trouble or fighting, is a suspicious faith;
for true faith is a fighting, wrestling faith.*

RALPH ERSKINE
"Stability in the Faith, the Church's Strength"

If you recognize that the Enemy may be at work in your home as you love a child with a traumatic past, be prepared to wield God's weapons. Along with the armor of God described in Ephesians 6, Scripture shows us that God's people also battled the Enemy with praise and worship.

PRAISE AND WORSHIP

Imagine the US Army on a battlefield, armed with long-range sniper rifles, powerful machine guns, and tanks able to survive nuclear, biological, and chemical attacks. Imagine the soldier with his M4 carbine, portable GPS receiver, and night-vision goggles.

Now imagine a group of soldiers marching on the front line of that battle, armed with only their voices. What are they doing? They're singing songs of praise and worship to God!

It sounds insane, but when Judah's king Jehoshaphat battled "a great multitude" (2 Chronicles 20:2), the Levites went first, singing and praising the God of Israel. The king was smart enough to know they couldn't face their enemies with merely human forces. So in anticipation of the battle, he and the people of Judah fasted and prayed together. After humbly admitting that he didn't have the answer to their problem, the king cried out to God, saying, "We do not know what to do, but our eyes are on you" (verse 12).

God answered through the Levite Jahaziel: "Do not be afraid and do not be dismayed at this great horde, for the battle is not yours but God's" (verse 15).

When the people heard this, they worshipped God, and the Levites stood up and praised Him in "a very loud voice" (verse 19). But the praise didn't stop there. The king talked it over with the people and appointed men to sing at the head of their army.

"When they began to sing and praise, the LORD set an ambush against the men of Ammon, Moab, and Mount Seir, who had come against Judah, so that they were routed" (verse 22).

The battle plan was fasting and praying together in humility and then facing their enemies by singing and praising God. The Bible says that God inhabits the praises of His people (Psalm 22:3), so I can imagine the presence of the Almighty on that battlefield. He was there as the singers marched toward the armies that were set to destroy them.

We can have the same battle plan. What a God we have! Praise and worship are powerful.

THE SWORD OF THE SPIRIT

I wish I had known to wield the weapon of praise on a daily basis when I struggled during that stressful first year with Daniel. I did rely on God's Word—it helped to write Scripture on index cards and place them everywhere—by my alarm clock, in the bathroom, on the stove, above the kitchen sink, and on the dash-board of the car. I needed God's Word constantly before me. I needed to read it over and over again, say it aloud, memorize it, and claim its truth.

For a time before and after the adoption, we were in a finan-cial bind. I remember a week of anxiety and sleepless nights, when I fretted about how we would pay all of our bills. One night as I lay awake in my bed, the Lord reminded me of Ephesians 6:10: "Be strong in the Lord and in his mighty power" (NIV). After I read and reread the armor-of-God verses in that chapter, I had no problem bringing them to mind whenever I started to become anxious. God's Word sustained me. I discovered that I had to be alert and take a stand against Satan, who would prefer that I be worried and sleepless.

I also taught Daniel to use God's Word as a weapon. One week I had him memorize John 14:6: "I am the way, and the truth, and the life. No one comes to the Father except through me." After waking up from a nightmare, he said this verse aloud and told me, "Hey, I feel better!"

Scripture was a lifeline for another adoptive mom when she found herself battling despair. Ann's teenage son—who had been adopted as an infant after being born with drugs in his system—was struggling with depression. He was skipping school and disappearing for days, and even more troubling, he sometimes became violent. The family worried that he would hurt himself or someone else.

"So finally we ended up having to put him in residential care, which is the last thing we ever wanted to do," Ann says. "For a child who has come from a broken family, who has already had that feeling of being rejected by a parent, the last thing you want to do is send him away. But we felt like we couldn't keep him safe and couldn't keep our other kids safe."

During that time, Ann felt she was in "a dark place. I would read my Bible, and I would just feel a black wall. Often when you read Scripture and have been praying, you sense God's presence, but it just wasn't there."

Thankfully, Ann's parents and a couple of close friends were praying for the family. And Ann continued to pray, even in the midst of darkness. One day she felt God speak to her.

You need to memorize Scripture, He told her.

Ann thought that idea sounded impossible and told God so. *You've got to be kidding! I'm barely coping. I'm barely managing. I'm reading Your Word, and nothing's there. How can I memorize it?*

God didn't argue with her but prompted her to open her Bible. As Ann started paging through the Word, she came to Psalm 57.

"I sensed God saying, *I want you to memorize Psalm 57.*"

That still sounded impossible to Ann, but she wrote the entire psalm on index cards and put them where she could see the verses during her daily routine. Slowly she began memorizing all eleven verses.

"At first, honestly, I was wondering if I heard God right," she recalls. "It didn't seem to be working for me, and it still felt like I was in a black hole. But as I began to get the verses down—it probably took three or four weeks—I started to sense God's presence there. And His truth took hold in my mind: *God is here.*"

Be gracious to me, O God,
be gracious to me,
For my soul takes refuge in You;
And in the shadow of Your wings
I will take refuge
Until destruction passes by.
I will cry to God Most High,
To God who accomplishes
all things for me.
He will send from heaven
and save me;
He reproaches him
who tramples upon me.
God will send forth His
lovingkindness and His truth. . . .
I will give thanks to You, O Lord,
among the peoples;
I will sing praises to You
among the nations.
For Your lovingkindness
is great to the heavens
And Your truth to the clouds.
Be exalted above the heavens, O God;
Let Your glory be above all the earth.

Psalm 57:1-3, 9-11, NASB

Notice that when Ann recited Psalm 57, she was singing praises to God, even in her darkness. Was God saying, *Praise Me, and you'll sense My presence*? As she memorized that psalm, she *was* praising Him. In fact, as she recited Psalm 57 while telling me this story, I strongly felt God's presence even then.

At the time Ann memorized this Scripture, she and her husband still weren't sure how long their son would need to be in residential care. Despite that fact, Ann recalls, "it felt like there was light in the darkness. As I let God's Word settle into my heart and mind, it made all the difference."

After nine months of treatment, Ann's son returned home. At the residential care facility, the staff was able to stabilize the teen's depression with the right medication and needed therapy, which he often missed at home because he would run away. Ann is convinced the stay saved her son's life. Today he's a stable young man who works full-time and has become more receptive to hearing from God.

Ann notes that she learned two lessons from that time:

1. Not to give up but to continue seeking after God, and
2. God's Word is a powerful tool in spiritual warfare.

"The big takeaway is to really work on hiding God's Word in your heart—letting God's Word do that work of spiritual battle," Ann says. "Second, keep finding different creative ways to hear from God and to fill your life with His presence."

Joining prayer groups, listening to an audio recording of the Bible in the car or as you go to sleep, posting Scripture on Pinterest, listening to Scripture set to music, subscribing to daily Scripture emails, and using adult coloring books filled with Scripture are all ways people have surrounded themselves with God's Word.

Perhaps your family won't face such struggles. If not, praise God! If you do, praise God anyway, and sing and speak His Word as a weapon against the Enemy. I'll admit that it's easier said than done, but battles aren't known to be easy.

God has already triumphed over Satan through Jesus' death on the cross, so let's praise Him aloud as the angels do in heaven:

> Holy, holy, holy, is the Lord God Almighty,
>   who was and is and is to come!
>
> Worthy are you, our Lord and God,
>   to receive glory and honor and power,
> for you created all things,
>   and by your will they existed and were created.

REVELATION 4:8, 11

THE SHIELD OF FAITH

Ephesians 6 reminds us of another important weapon we can employ as we battle Satan: the shield of faith. If we hold up our shield, we can "extinguish all the flaming darts of the evil one" (verse 16).

Jessamy and Jeff Johnson are an example of adoptive parents who have raised their shield of faith again and again, praying and trusting God to provide for, protect, and continue the healing process in the four children they've adopted from the foster-care system. And God has never failed them.

As the Johnsons faced an especially difficult struggle with one of their children a few years ago, God gave Jessamy a powerful vision of how their faith and prayers shield their children from Satan's attacks. The family was at church at the time, and Jessamy was singing and worshipping God when He gave her the vision she later recorded in her journal:

I saw myself standing before God and in the midst of His faithful people. My legs were planted firmly, my body tall and confident as I grasped the strong hand of my husband, standing firmly and confidently beside me. Heads raised, faces forward, muscles tensed, the two of us formed a shield for our four adopted children behind us.

In front of us, the enemy was writhing, pushing forward, striving to get our children. My eyes saw darkness and bursts of red volcanic explosions, flashes of light, and images of anger, violence, and horror coming at us in waves. Our feet were firm, cemented to the spot where we stood, and we leaned ever so slightly forward, ready to absorb the blows.

Weapons were raised against us, accusations and lies hurled toward us. I readied myself for the pain, searing heat, slashes, blows—whatever would come. I stared straight forward, and from the corner of my eye could see my husband doing the same—resolute, unfazed by the hordes of evil beings sneering and threatening.

I was not afraid. I was ready. We were ready. We were calm, prepared for the onslaught. We knew our children were safe behind us—not because we were about to protect them but because we, as temples of the living God, were empowered by God's Spirit to intercede for them and be the means by which He redeems them and brings them to His glorious light.

What Satan intended for evil in their lives—neglect, malnutrition, violence, abuse, loneliness, lies that they are worthless, unwanted, without hope—God has purposed to turn for good.

He has called us to stand for them. He has equipped us as their parents to march against the gates of hell, to

shoulder what we can of their pain, to share what we can
of their deep and unspeakable sorrow. We feel bruised and
battered, emptied and abused, but we stand. We stand with
them now behind us, now behind Him whose promises are
yes and amen. We stand and they are safe.

The enemy has no power to fog their minds with
malicious whispers about who they "really are" or remind
them where they came from and suggest they will return
there. We will fight until the battle is over. We will absorb
the attacks of the evil one who roams the earth looking for
those he can devour and whose aim is to steal, kill, and
destroy.

We will stand so that our children can stand. We
will stand so that as they see us armed with our faith
and the power of our great God, they will experience His
redemption from the inside out and begin to walk in the
same power available to them as they journey into who God
has destined them to be.

I don't know if God is reminding me that I've stood
through attacks before and I can stand again, or [is]
preparing me for a new round. But I know that I will
stand. I know that the devil is defeated. I know whom I
have believed—that He is faithful, and that my children
are in His care.

Jessamy tells me that this vision continues to be a source of
strength for her. Let it also be a source of strength for you, a visual
reminder of your position in the spiritual realm.

As the Johnsons do, put on the complete armor of God, and
then stand firm. The Amplified Bible says that as you do this,
"you will be able to [successfully] resist and stand your ground
in the evil day [of danger], and having done everything [that

the crisis demands], to stand firm [in your place, fully prepared, immovable, victorious]" (Ephesians 6:13).

Rest Stop

Read Matthew 4:1-11 and consider how Jesus battled Satan in the wilderness. Read and study Ephesians 6, asking God to open your eyes to "see wonderful things" in His Word (Psalm 119:18, TLB). Before your next prayer time, play your favorite praise music and sing to God. And then ask the Lord if there are specific Scriptures He wants you to memorize and add to your arsenal so you can keep your family strong. Record those and other meaningful Scriptures on the journal page, along with any strategies you'll employ—or have employed—to resist Satan.

My Journey to Adoption

DATE _____

Sing to God, sing praises to his name; lift up
a song to him who rides through the deserts;
his name is the LORD; exult before him!

Psalm 68:4

CHAPTER 15

Forgiveness

*Every one says forgiveness is a lovely idea,
until they have something to forgive.*

C. S. LEWIS
Mere Christianity

If you adopt and care for a child who has experienced trauma and loss, you may find yourself learning about forgiveness in new ways.

While every family is a petri dish for learning the lessons of forgiveness, adoption seems to provide additional reasons to forgive. You and your child may need to forgive your child's birth parents. You may need to forgive each other when trauma behaviors or other adoption issues cause division in your home. You may need to forgive someone in the foster-care system or a relative who doesn't offer support when you need it. Finally, you may need to forgive yourself because you've fallen short as a parent in a way you never could have imagined.

Forgiveness isn't easy, but our goal as parents should be to model it for our kids. Some of these children will have a difficult battle ahead of them to forgive their birth parents or people who hurt them. Fortunately, Jesus has shown us the path to forgiveness through His own perfect example.

FORGIVING RELATIVES

Let's say you welcome a child into your home who was sexually abused for years. Or you discover your toddler was duct-taped to his crib and left alone for a day. Or your little girl's brain has been damaged because she was exposed to drugs or alcohol as a fetus. How will you feel about the people who hurt your child?

"I've had a lot of anger in the past toward birth parents and anyone who has abused any of my children," says Laura, an adoptive mother of four. "I know they need Christ, but at first I felt hatred for the people who hurt my daughter. You can feel that way when you find out something so horrific has been done to your child. But I had to learn to forgive."

Resentment toward birth parents can also raise its ugly head when *you* are the one dealing with the difficult task of helping a hurt child heal from wounds someone else inflicted, she adds.

Adoptive and foster mom Irene Garcia notes that at one point, she also harbored resentment toward her children's birth parents.

"How ugly!" she says. "I was being compassionate to those I thought were worthy of my compassion—the orphans, not the parents. I really thought I could justify my feelings because orphans were needy and depended on our help."

The birth mother of two of Irene's children kidnapped a child, abused him, and then threw him out the window when the police arrived on the scene.

"In my mind, she didn't deserve my forgiveness," Irene confesses. "I started to get self-righteous. Here I was rescuing these children from evil. God would certainly agree with my hate-filled heart, right?"

A RUDE AWAKENING

Irene faced a rude awakening when she found herself speaking to her daughter Elaine about forgiving her birth mother. "A flood of guilt rushed through my veins," she recalls. "Who am I? My sin was no different from this birth mom's. That was when I came face-to-face with my sin—an unforgiving heart. God doesn't measure sin—it's all dark and evil to Him. My goal should be to share the gospel with these broken people. They need Christ too!"

Today Irene and her husband, Domingo, encourage other foster and adoptive parents to put themselves in biological parents' shoes.

"How would you feel toward a person who is taking your kids away?" Irene asks. "As hard as it is, we need to feel the pain many of these mamas feel." Irene recognized that she had once viewed her children's birth parents as the enemy. Yet she knew that even legitimate enemies require our love if we're to follow Jesus' commandments.

John and Terri Moore also found it easy at first to vilify the birth relatives of their children, in part because they were afraid the children would love their biological parents more than they loved them. John says they planned to "keep a healthy distance" from the birth relatives once the adoptions were finalized. Even so, about ten months after bringing their boys home, they found themselves meeting with their sons' maternal grandmother.

"Within minutes of meeting this woman, we had fallen in love with her," John recalls. "God softened our hearts, and because of His work in us, we now have wonderful relationships with many of our children's birth families.

"When Jesus calls us to love our neighbors, that includes the birth relatives of the children we adopt. They, too, are made in the image of God. And while it's easy to judge someone who has perhaps abused, neglected, or abandoned a child, we don't know his or her story. This person may have experienced similar treatment growing up."

While the Moores have ground rules for ongoing contact with biological relatives in order to keep their children from any type of distress, the connections they've made have helped their children with their own journeys of forgiveness and healing. John writes,

> Continued contact with birth relatives can be healthy for a child if done right. It can lessen the sense of loss and grief, it can provide opportunities for questions to be answered, and it can provide opportunities for a child to extend grace and forgiveness.
>
> These days, one of our son's birth fathers comes to all his football games, sitting with us and high-fiving me whenever our son does anything noteworthy. "It's in the genes, buddy!" he jokingly reminds me.
>
> One of our daughter's birth fathers comes to our church semiregularly, arriving early and saving seats. Another daughter's birth parents meet us in the park just to hang out. Not only were our fears unfounded, but we've also been incredibly blessed as we've welcomed these relationships into our lives.
>
> Our children have been blessed as well, witnessing love and grace in relationships where mistrust and fear all too often take root. They are able to forever avoid the guilt many kids feel when they feel torn between their love for their adoptive parents and their birth relatives. Moreover, they have seen God bring healing and

reconciliation to broken lives and relationships, and they have been blessed to be a part of that healing.

MODELING FORGIVENESS

In chapter 12, I shared how the Lord had taught me to deepen my trust in Him during our difficult first year with Daniel. At the same time, I was learning about forgiveness.

It had been seven months since Daniel became our son. We were going to therapy with him, trying to help him feel safe and loved and working to help him express his feelings of anger and loss. I read that it could be a healing activity to playact younger developmental stages with children who may not have experienced those stages in a healthy way. So I purchased baby toys and brought out the baby blankets, and we "played baby" a few times. Daniel loved the baby talk and the cuddling.

But there were still many difficult days in our home when Daniel's anger would throw us all for a loop. In fact, the bad days outnumbered the good days. We didn't know how to deal with his behavior.

One day Daniel flew into a rage because his older sister was allowed to use the computer twice, and he wasn't. He wouldn't listen to my explanation: She needed the computer for homework, not fun. His rages were irrational, and when he was in that state, he simply couldn't listen.

Jeff came home to this scene, with Daniel ranting and raving, sounding for the world like a two-year-old having a tantrum. He decided to tape-record Daniel in this state so he could play it back for him when he calmed down. He thought it would teach him a lesson.

It was a bad strategy. Daniel grew even angrier when he saw the tape recorder and realized what my husband was doing.

Grabbing the recorder, Daniel dropped it on the floor and then took out the batteries.

Jeff asked for the batteries, but Daniel wouldn't give them back. By this time, Jeff was angry too. I'd seen my husband become truly angry only a few times in twenty years of marriage, but even my calm husband had his breaking point. As he grabbed Daniel to retrieve the batteries, I moved closer to both of them.

Feeling trapped by the two of us—and still enraged—Daniel turned around as he tried to free himself and swung his fist in my direction. He ended up punching me squarely in the chest.

I was shocked.

"He hit me!" I cried.

Jeff managed to safely put his body over Daniel's to contain him until he calmed down.

I was anything but calm. I continued to cry as I managed to drive our three other children to church for their youth-group meeting. I didn't stay at church but drove the fifteen minutes back home, sobbing all the way and trying to make sense of what had happened.

What kind of world was I living in? This type of thing didn't happen in my home! This wasn't my family!

I felt a foreign emotion rising in my injured chest—it was shame. I was ashamed that my son had hit me. Because of this experience, I had a taste of how horrible shame can feel. I'm sure Daniel had felt that emotion many times when he was hurt at the orphanage.

Needless to say, we learned from that incident how to better handle our son when his anger became irrational. Keep calm. Don't corner him. Don't argue or talk. I wish I'd been wise enough to just turn on some praise music and start praying the moment these fits of rage occurred.

After Daniel calmed down that night, he told Jeff that I would never forgive him. I went through the motions, praying with him and telling him that I did forgive him. I knew that forgiving him was the right thing to do, that forgiveness was a choice. But I was hurt. Deep down, I was still angry with this boy whose world had been in chaos his entire life. I hadn't totally forgiven this traumatized kid who had lived with us only seven months, who was learning a new language, who was full of anxiety and wondering if he could trust these people who were supposedly going to be his "forever" family. I was offended, and my chest ached. I even thought of going to a doctor, but I was too ashamed to tell him what had happened.

Four days later, on a Sunday morning, I flunked the forgiveness test. Jeff and I were beginning to recognize a pattern. For some reason, Sundays were a very bad day for Daniel. I sensed Satan was on the attack. As we were getting ready for church, Daniel started acting oppositional again, and I wasn't happy with that.

"Daniel, why do you have to be so angry?" And then I mentioned how he had hit me. "My chest still hurts, you know."

"But I thought you forgave me" was my son's heartbreaking reply.

Part of me must have wanted to punish him. It was obvious I hadn't forgiven him. Psalm 103:12 says, "As far as the east is from the west, so far does [Christ] remove our transgressions from us," but I was holding Daniel's transgression close.

At church that morning, God reminded me during the sermon that throwing Daniel's offense in his face was not forgiveness. *How can you expect Daniel to forgive his birth father and mother, and all the people who hurt him, if you can't forgive him for this one thing?*

At that moment I realized the immense task that lay before Daniel. Convicted by the Father who had forgiven me of everything, I asked Daniel to forgive me for bringing the matter up again.

FORGIVING YOURSELF

As you grapple with forgiveness and seek to model it for your child, don't forget that you may also need to forgive yourself. Sometimes the wounds of your child can bring out the worst in you, and it's not a pretty picture.

One day, just before we adopted our kids, I was reading my Bible when a passage jumped from the page. It was obvious that the Holy Spirit wanted me to pay attention to Jeremiah 18:1-6:

> This is the word that came to Jeremiah from the LORD:
> "Go down to the potter's house, and there I will give
> you my message." So I went down to the potter's house,
> and I saw him working at the wheel. But the pot he was
> shaping from the clay was marred in his hands; so the
> potter formed it into another pot, shaping it as seemed
> best to him.
>
> Then the word of the LORD came to me. He said,
> "Can I not do with you, Israel, as this potter does?"
> declares the LORD. "Like clay in the hand of the potter,
> so are you in my hand, Israel." (NIV)

Lord, I asked, *why do You need to smash my pot? I'm doing what You've asked. We're adopting the kids.* Was I really that bad that He needed to mold a new pot? A new me? I couldn't see that I required reshaping.

Now when I think of that time, I'm astounded at how self-righteous and blind I was. During that first stressful year with Daniel, I saw how much my heart needed remodeling. I'm reminded of one of those HGTV shows where a couple strips the interior of a house down to the studs before rebuilding. God needed to show me all the mold, cracks, and filth in my heart. That year I said and did many hurtful things in anger; I had sinful attitudes; I nearly gave up on God. I saw my sin and its ugliness as I never had before. I found myself lying prostrate before God, broken and humbled.

In his book *Total Forgiveness*, Pastor R. T. Kendall talks about how Christians often "rate" sin:

> God knows not only the sins we have committed but also the sins of which we are capable. He knows our hearts. He sees what is deep down inside that we may not be willing to face. Our self-righteousness and personal sense of decency often camouflage the evil that is within our soul. When the Bible says in 1 John 1:7 that Jesus' blood purifies from *all sin*, it means we have been forgiven even for sins we weren't aware of. The truth is, given the right circumstances, pressure, temptation, and timing, *any* of us can match the evil . . . we ourselves have to forgive.[1]

With the right pressure, temptation, and timing, I could have been an alcoholic like Daniel's mother or committed any number of sins. Living with a hurt child who felt a subconscious need to recreate a constant atmosphere of chaos was difficult for me. It required patience, self-control, selflessness, and humility to a degree that revealed my impatience, lack of self-control, selfishness, and pride. It revealed the sin in my heart as nothing had before.

"I didn't realize how sinful I was until I adopted children," I told another adoptive mom. When I told her this, she gasped— because she felt the same way.

Blogger Brandy Lee, who adopted an eighteen-month-old, observes that adoption, like marriage, can expose our darkest sins. "My sinful response to adoption was shocking, most of all to myself," she writes. "I never expected to struggle with such anger and frustration."[2]

There may be days—or months—when you're appalled by your own sinful heart as you become the target of your child's pain. You might see the worst of yourself as your child's withdrawn or aggressive behavior continues to greet you each day, whether or not you're ready for it. You may see your capacity for selfishness, for protecting yourself, for seeking comfort. Consider this viewpoint a gift from God. With it, He can move you away from self-righteousness and toward deeper repentance and humility.

God wants us to mourn over our sin—to cry, weep, and be broken by it. In fact, when Jesus said in the Beatitudes, "Blessed are those who mourn, for they shall be comforted" (Matthew 5:4), He was talking about mourning sin, not death.[3]

Yet once we deal with the seriousness of our sin, "there is hope in the here and now," wrote the late Jerry Bridges in *The Blessing of Humility*. Like David, we can say, "My sacrifice, O God, is a broken spirit; a broken and contrite heart you, God, will not despise" (Psalm 51:17, NIV).

"If we are repentant, we can take that sin to the Cross and experience immediate forgiveness," Bridges said. "We can experience the truth that God will not count that sin against us; He will not despise a broken and contrite heart."[4]

If you find yourself broken by your own sin as you parent a child with a traumatic past, know that this is all part of God's inner-remodeling plan.

In *Walking with God through Pain and Suffering*, Timothy Keller writes,

We have many blemishes in our character. We are too fragile under criticism or too harsh in giving it. We are bad listeners, or ungenerous to people we think foolish, or too impulsive, or too timid and cowardly, or too controlling, or unreliable. But we are largely blind to these things. . . .

Then suffering comes along. Timidity and cowardice, selfishness and self-pity, tendencies toward bitterness and dishonesty—all of these "impurities" of soul are revealed and drawn out by trials and suffering just as a furnace draws the impurities out of unrefined metal ore. Finally we can see who we really are. Like fire working on gold, suffering can destroy some things within us and can purify and strengthen other things.

Or not. It depends on our response.[5]

If you're surprised by the mold and mildew of sin in your inner home and need to seek your child's forgiveness as well as God's, don't continue to condemn yourself as Satan would have you do. Remember, God desires restoration, not condemnation. He wants to replace the broken tiles and strengthen the beams of your soul.

So assist the Lord with your makeover. Be willing to believe in Him, even in the mess of demolition. Walk next to Jesus, hauling out the broken floorboards, smashing the walls that are no longer needed. Be willing to turn to Him, to depend on Him, knowing that His loving hands are ready to install the new hardwood floors and granite countertops—solid, long-lasting updates to your inner home. Demolition is ugly, but the process is necessary if you want a stronger, more beautiful house—and soul.

As missionary Jim Elliot wrote, "Most laws condemn the soul and pronounce sentence. . . . The result of the law of my God is perfect. It condemns but forgives. . . . It restores—more than abundantly—what it takes away."[6]

Be determined to continually model forgiveness and restoration for your child, realizing that one day, he or she may face the herculean task of forgiving others for abuse or abandonment. Show your child the path to peace.

ⓘ Rest Stop

Corrie ten Boom once said, "Forgiveness is an act of the will, and the will can function regardless of the temperature of the heart."[7] What's the temperature of your heart regarding areas where forgiveness is needed? Read Matthew 6:14-15, Mark 11:25, Luke 11:4, and Luke 17:4. How do these verses support Corrie ten Boom's assertion that forgiveness begins with a choice, not a feeling? How can you exercise your will today regarding forgiveness? Record your thoughts on the journal page.

My Journey to Adoption

DATE _____

Be kind to one another, tenderhearted, forgiving
one another, as God in Christ forgave you.

Ephesians 4:32

CHAPTER 16

The Healing Path

[Christ] was pierced for our transgressions, he was crushed for
our iniquities; the punishment that brought us peace was
on him, and by his wounds we are healed.

ISAIAH 53:5, NIV

We all desire complete healing for children who have suffered wounds of abandonment or abuse. While our love and care for our children can—and often does—bring about astounding transformations, a tension exists between our hopes and prayers and the knowledge that the healing of bodies and minds is not guaranteed while we live in this world.

So how do we deal with that tension? First, we remember that God is the only One who understands the mystery of healing. As we faithfully do what we can to help our children, we must also submit to God's sovereignty and leave what we can't understand in His compassionate hands.

God says in Isaiah 55:9, "As the heavens are higher than the earth, so are my ways higher than your ways and my thoughts than your thoughts." But there are days when we don't especially like the fact that God's thoughts are not our thoughts. We want answers, and we want them now.

When your new child cries so long and hard that the nursery attendant at church turns you away, you want healing—*fast*. When your new little ones are touching and hugging you and hanging on you around the clock—and it's been that way for more than a year—you want healing *now*.

THE ULTIMATE HEALING

Have you ever wondered why Jesus didn't physically heal every sick and wounded person in Israel when He was there in human form? Just think about it: He easily could have done so.

While He healed many people of physical ailments while on earth (and continues to do so), His Father's goal for sending His Son was to provide the ultimate healing for all of humankind, a healing that comes through the salvation and eternal life available only in Christ. While Jesus was on this side of heaven, He was simply obeying His Father, and so must we.

Here's how I grapple with the issue of healing in my limited brain: I know that sometimes God chooses to heal people in certain ways while they're on this sinful planet, and sometimes He waits to heal people completely in heaven.

As you welcome children with wounds and losses into your life, it's important to realize that you—a mere mortal—don't have power to heal every fiber of their being. But you *can* lead them to Jesus, who can offer them the ultimate healing that will last for eternity. When a three-year-old throws outrageous emotional fits all day long and then later says, "Mommy, I want to ask Jesus into my heart," the result is healing that will last forever.

A GOOD DAY

Little by little, Daniel's anxiety began to lessen. One morning, almost exactly a year after we brought him home from Russia, he walked into the kitchen and simply expressed his feelings instead of acting out and becoming angry with me for no reason.

"Mom, I need a hug," he said. "I feel crabby."

The next day he told me, "Mom, I feel grumpy." And he *came to me* for a hug. This was major progress, and so much easier to live with than oppositional behavior.

And then, on a beautiful Indian summer day, Daniel decided to trust Jeff and me. He had responded normally to just about everything that day—there had been none of his usual attempts to get under my skin. We were sitting on the dock in our back-yard, watching the sunfish dart about in the lake.

"I've had a good day," he said to me.

"Yeah, you have! How come?"

"Well, I just decided to."

And that was it. For us, it was a miracle. Life became easier. Daniel became my thoughtful helper. "What else can I do for you, Mom?" he would ask. "Let me carry that for you—you don't want to hurt your back again," he would say as he grabbed a bag of groceries from my hands.

Almost two years after we brought Daniel home, he stopped becoming anxious if my mood changed slightly. Usually, any deviation in my facial expression, any tone of slight crabbiness or annoyance, or even my displeasure with something in a movie (rats, for instance) would trigger his anxiety because he thought something bad would happen. (I didn't understand this at the time, and it would have helped greatly to know. Seek a therapist's help, if needed, so you can understand the why behind certain behaviors as soon as possible.)

One day when I was a bit annoyed with one of the other kids, Daniel put his arms around me and said, "Mom, you need a hug." This was another miracle! He finally knew that my annoyance wasn't something to be afraid of. It didn't mean trauma was around the corner.

Two years after we adopted our new son, he made me a Mother's Day card with a message that brought tears to my eyes. "Thank you for being the best mom anyone could wish for," he wrote. "That really changed my life a lot."

Daniel became a great hugger and a real people person—a social, empathetic, talkative kid with a never-say-never attitude who loved riding his bike, helping his friends, lighting fireworks, heading a ball as hard as he could during a soccer game, and making people laugh.

TRY A PAUSE

As we try to help a child adjust to a new home and heal from early trauma, we can't expect to see straightforward progress from one day to the next. We're more apt to see our children take one step forward and then two steps back. At some point, they may seem to leave a certain behavior behind for good, only to revert to it in a time of stress.

As you zigzag with your child through the healing process, it helps to build in a ritual of pausing. Is there a certain time in the day when you can give your child, and yourself, a break from the difficult work of healing and growing emotionally? As a mother of children who had so much learning and catching up to do, it was easy for me to always be in the teach-them mode. Actually, I learned the value of the pause from my new children.

As Russians, Daniel and Masha were accustomed to drinking tea, and lots of it. Teatime was part of their culture. Even in the orphanage, they could count on having tea with sugar. So when the excitement of that first summer at our home died down and the hard of work of school in America began, Masha led me to the Russian tea set gathering dust on the living room shelf.

"Why no use?" she asked in her emerging English.

Good question! I thought as I suddenly realized it had been months since these children had tasted tea. The tea set represented more than a drink to them; it was something familiar—a comfort food, if you will.

So every day before they stepped off the school bus, I set the teapot, graced with lilacs and an iridescent shimmer, on our kitchen table and placed three matching teacups and saucers in their appropriate places. In the center of the trio was a plate of cookies, nuts, and other repasts.

As I poured the steaming water into the teapot, Masha and Daniel would walk in the door and heave a sigh of relief as they threw off their backpacks. Sitting at the table, they proceeded to stir sugar into their teacups, and then we sipped and slurped our tea as they told me (or tried to tell me) about their day.

It was a moment of calm, a time to take a deep breath. There was nothing at stake during this time, nothing to learn. It came after the business and stress of the day, but before any homework frustrations and emotional upheavals might occur.

My new kids were behind academically and struggling to learn English. Their losses were innumerable—I couldn't even replicate the Russian bread they loved. But at least now, when this new life seemed too overwhelming, there was always the safe haven of teatime.

I was surprised that the practice also became a calming ritual for me. As I tried to understand my new kids, to teach them to express their feelings and deal with their frustrations and anger, I also had times when I felt overwhelmed. I needed teatime too.

It was a friendly pause—a respite, a time-out—before we got

on with the hard business of life. Teatime helped me make it to bedtime prayers, when I often heard my new children pray, "And thank You, Jesus, for my family."

A SHOT AT LIFE

With seven broken bones, large whip marks, and ears that had been twisted so much they were purple, it was apparent that two-year-old Logan needed plenty of healing—physically and emotionally.

"He was bruised literally from head to feet," Amy says. "He had a bruise on his buttock that stayed for four months."

The toddler came into the world as a result of rape, and his mother left him with her alcoholic parents who also smoked pot. They abused Logan and left him to wander the streets. Amy and Brian thought the boy was autistic because he was withdrawn and emotionless and wouldn't make eye contact.

"But he wasn't autistic," Amy explains. "All he needed was love and attention, and then he became a normal, superkind little boy."

For almost two years, Amy and Brian loved little Logan as their foster son, with hopes of adopting him. If Logan needed to visit his birth mom, Amy spoke about it in positive terms; but Logan never wanted to go.

"How 'bout if I wait till tomorrow?" he would ask in his sweet four-year-old voice.

The visits became longer as the foster-care system worked to reunite the boy with his birth mom. Eventually, Amy, Brian, and their other children (several of whom had been adopted) had to say good-bye to Logan.

"I should have been a basket case by the last two months, not knowing if he would be with us or not," Amy says. "But I never really lost it. I trusted God. I didn't break down in front of Logan.

When I was younger, I would have. I definitely wouldn't have been able to control myself. Now I'm much more prepared in a Christlike way. I've had eight children, and I'm more trusting. I know God loves these kids and knows exactly where they should be."

Logan's birth mother is a young non-Christian who doesn't know much about being a mother, but she's learning.

"She listens, and that's rewarding in itself," Amy notes. "She calls me for advice all the time. She trusts me and likes me, and I love her. She needs Christ, and she needs a mother."

No matter what happens with Logan's future, Amy and Brian know that God gave them a chance to take part in a healing miracle.

"The wonderful thing about foster care is that we had the chance to be part of a transformation. Just the love of God, the love of parents, and the family giving him attention completely transformed Logan. And now he has a shot at life."

HEALING FOR PARENTS

Children with trauma in their past often develop survival skills. Dr. Karyn Purvis identified the five major ones as aggression, violence, manipulation, control, and triangulation (which means they're experts at pitting parents or two other people against each other).[1] These survival skills can wreak havoc on adoptive parents, causing wounds that can seem to sneak up on them after a lengthy time of exposure to their children's maladaptive behaviors.

After Daniel began to trust my husband and me, he started letting go of many of his survival skills. Life settled down. Without the constant crises in my home, I suddenly had a moment to reflect on myself. I felt terrible, like a shell of my former self. I found no pleasure in anything. I would be at my newspaper job and find myself crying in the bathroom for no apparent reason. I wanted to avoid people. I made sure the neighbors weren't around when I went outside my house. And then I started having panic attacks, also for no apparent reason.

What in the world is wrong with me? I wondered. *Daniel is finally healing, but I'm a mess!*

Our therapist said I most likely had what's called secondary or shadow trauma from dealing with Daniel's trauma-induced behavior. All I know is that I was physically, emotionally, and mentally exhausted after being exposed to more than a year of chronic stress and atypical circumstances in my home.

The label wasn't that important, but healing was. The panic attacks finally sent me to a doctor, and I discovered I was clinically depressed. Therapy and medication eventually helped me heal.

Don't be surprised if you, too, might need to seek healing for yourself, though you may not find yourself struggling with depression as I did, especially if you can learn a few things from my experience and mistakes. That's my prayer, in any case.

A FEW DON'TS

1. *Don't take vacations while your child is adjusting to you.* Six months after the adoption, Jeff and I took all our children, including our anxious new son, on a plane to California for a family get-together. This basically gave Daniel an invitation to become overwhelmed with fear. I also regret a summer camping trip to Mount Rushmore that first year, with all four children, in one-hundred-degree heat. I didn't sleep for three nights and spent three days trapped in a van with an anxious child who wanted to make me angry (and he did). A simplified routine during the adjustment period will make life easier on everyone.

2. *Don't talk too much and pray too little, as I did.* One survival skill children coming from hard places may use is control with manipulation. If they can engage you in an argument, you can be manipulated. If you keep your mouth shut until you have time to consider how to respond—or *whether* you should—it's harder for this to happen, and it's harder for emotions to escalate.

3. *Don't label yourself a failure if at some point your child needs out-of-home care.* I know several loving Christian parents who had to use out-of-home care for the health and safety of their child, as well as for the safety of the rest of the family. Your child may have needs you cannot meet in your home. Mental disorders are as real as cancer. Parents need to take their child to a hospital to treat cancer, and you may need to take your child elsewhere to treat a mental disorder.

4. *Don't forget that your biological children may also need some healing if your new child's behaviors have been difficult.* Don't be so intent on "fixing" your new child that you forget your biological children, whose needs may not seem as urgent. If you're struggling, they're probably struggling too. Are they depressed? Do they feel safe? Do they feel as if they need to be perfect and not bother you because the adopted child has so many needs? Are there warnings signs, such as dropping grades or changes in demeanor? Do your birth children need your attention?

A FEW DOS

1. *Assume that your child will most likely need help beyond what you can provide.* That way, you'll be more open to

seeking help sooner rather than later, if it's needed. Prepare yourself by researching therapists in your area who understand adoption issues. The earlier you have help with attachment strategies and assistance with any behavioral mysteries, the better.

2. *Realize that you'll need to help your new child feel safe in your home.* Learn about the body's flight, fight, or freeze responses to fear and stress. Your child may be freezing, fighting, or fleeing because something in the environment seems threatening to him or her. Your tone of voice, or something that reminds your child of past abuse, may initiate this fear response. I didn't realize until much later that Daniel reacted to stress by fighting (acting out) and fleeing (running away), and Masha reacted by freezing. Realizing that your children are reacting in these ways because it's the only way they know how to cope with stress will keep you from seeing their behavior as disrespectful or defiant.

3. *If you take things personally, take them straight to God.* Experts say that you need to separate yourself from your child's trauma behaviors and act in a matter-of-fact way. "Don't take things personally," we're told. If the child is acting toward you in a way that feels disrespectful, hurtful, and offensive, it's not about you. This is true, and being matter-of-fact works.

Here was my problem: Sometimes I could act that way, but many times I couldn't. I learned to have a love-hate relationship with the "Don't take it personally" phrase. I'm not alone. Many adoptive parents have a hard time with this as well, especially if they're facing difficult behavior on a 24/7 basis.

So I would add, "If you take things personally, take

them straight to God." If your child copes by pushing your buttons, ignoring you, or manipulating you, and you feel the need to say something, tell yourself that you can only talk to God in that moment—not your child.

If that seems too difficult to do immediately, try repeating the names of God and truths about Him to calm yourself and move the focus to Him: "He is the Alpha and the Omega, the beginning and the end; the Prince of Peace; the Lord of Lords; He is my Provider, my Refuge, and my ever-present Help in time of need—His love never fails." As you do this, you'll bring God into the moment of frustration and model for your child a new way to cope.

A therapist's tip also helped me not to take things personally, ending Daniel's verbal attacks on me. The therapist suggested putting on headphones and listening to music when Daniel's intent was to pester me until I lost my temper. Before I put on the headphones, I would tell Daniel that I'd be happy to talk to him when he could address me respectfully. All he had to do was tap me on the shoulder, and I would take off the headphones and listen to him. When he realized he could no longer incite my anger this way, he stopped trying.

4. *Remember that healing can be an ongoing process.* Stay alert at different stages in a child's development and during major life changes. High school graduation, moving, or other changes can bring abandonment issues to the forefront.

You may adopt a child as an infant and have no concerns until adolescence hits. Then, seemingly out of the blue, your child may begin struggling with adoption issues as he or she tries to piece together an identity. One component of adolescent development is the search for identity, which can be a more complex task for children who were adopted than for children raised in birth families.

BUT IF NOT . . .

When Shadrach, Meshach, and Abednego walked into the fiery furnace because they refused to bow down to King Nebuchadnezzar, they recognized God's sovereignty.

While they knew that God was able to save them, they also realized that He could do as He willed. So they told the king, "Our God whom we serve is able to deliver us from the burning fiery furnace, and he will deliver us out of your hand, O king. *But if not*, be it known to you, O king, that we will not serve your gods or worship the golden image that you have set up" (Daniel 3:17-18, emphasis added).

This is a stance we can emulate as we seek healing for children with difficult beginnings. We can do our best to find appropriate therapies and parenting strategies to help our children heal as they grow. We can pray fervently for them; we can ask church elders to anoint them with oil and pray for them (James 5:14); we can cry out for miracles and point our children to Jesus and their ultimate healing in heaven. And we can tell ourselves that God is able to heal here on earth, *but if He doesn't*, we must remain faithful servants to our sovereign Lord.

If it seems that your child may have long-lasting scars from wounds of the past, consider Robert Kellemen's words: "In this life, your scar may not go away, but neither will His. He understands. He cares. He's there."[2]

🖊 *Rest Stop* ....

If your child is struggling, don't hesitate to ask your Father for a miracle and seek prayer from church elders. At the same time, don't hesitate to seek professional help. Numerous therapies are available that can make a positive difference, and researchers will discover more as they continue to gain knowledge about the human mind and body. Pray that God will lead you to resources that will benefit your child. Write your prayers on the journal page, and don't forget to listen for answers.

My Journey to Adoption

DATE _____

Let us then with confidence draw near to the
throne of grace, that we may receive mercy
and find grace to help in time of need.

Hebrews 4:16

CHAPTER 17

Worth the Risk

*As a prisoner for the Lord, then, I urge you to live
a life worthy of the calling you have received.*

EPHESIANS 4:1, NIV

Eight months after the adoption, I found myself struggling with Daniel's behaviors and wondering if the chaos affecting everyone in our family was worth it. Anna tried to find every reason to be away from home so she could avoid the craziness; Ben was frustrated with Daniel's behavior, telling him to "just respect Mom"; Masha tried to bring peace after Daniel's outbursts by offering me pictures she had drawn; and my husband and I found ourselves being critical of each other.

I couldn't understand why God was allowing this turmoil in our family to go on and on. Then one day while I was at church, He gave me an answer through Romans 8:17: "Since we are [God's] children, we will share his treasures—for all God gives to his Son Jesus is now ours too. *But if we are to share his glory, we must also share his suffering*" (TLB, emphasis added).

Suddenly the truth slammed into my heart: This pain was a normal part of a Christian's life! Somehow, in this situation, I was sharing in Christ's sufferings, and it was part of the plan. How had I missed this? Or had my head knowledge suddenly transformed to heart knowledge? Simply realizing this truth was a huge relief. It helped me understand and endure. As our pastor preached on grace that day, Jesus more clearly opened my eyes to the plan: I was taking in pain, but I was to give out grace, just as He had done. I felt honored to go through this trial for Christ's sake.

Was that year or so of duress in our household worth the suffering? During that time, two souls entered God's kingdom; two children experienced the love, health, and safety they desperately needed; and I grew closer to God as He shaped and molded me to be more like Him. Yes, it was worth it.

I'm not the only adoptive parent who will say that obeying God's call to adopt, despite any hardships involved, is more than worthwhile. In the previous chapter, I told you about how Amy and her family spent almost two years caring for Logan and watching him heal, and yet they had to let him go.

For those considering adoption or foster care, Amy has this advice:

> Remember Romans 8:18. There are things you are going to suffer: how the kids treat you, the problems they bring along, the way your family is affected when you are first adjusting to a new child. But it's all worth it later when you look back. Even losing Logan was worth it. It's all worth it. We do suffer in many different ways, yet our life is a mist. It passes so fast! It's a dash—the one between the birth and death date—and what matters is what we do with the dash.

Whatever Jesus calls us to do, obeying Him is always worth it. *Always.*

STRUGGLING AGAIN

As Daniel entered his senior year of high school at age nineteen, the old anxiety returned. He wondered what would happen to him when he graduated from high school. Would he have to move away? Would he have to figure out his future all alone?

We worked on a plan, finding a course of study that interested him at a nearby technical college. This way, he could continue to live at home. We assured him that we would always be his parents, that graduating didn't mean he would be on his own. He seemed relieved.

Yet that winter, he always seemed to be irritable and on edge. One night he looked incredibly sad and told me he couldn't sleep. He never felt happy, and now even helping his friends didn't make him feel better. He didn't feel like eating or doing anything. I recognized the symptoms of clinical depression, and I was worried. Depression was serious business, especially considering Daniel's past. I talked to him about how depression can run in families, how certain people can be genetically predisposed to it, but medication and therapy can help. We prayed together, and the next morning I took him to the doctor.

"Have you had thoughts of hurting yourself?" the doctor asked him.

"Yes," my son said.

"Do you have a specific plan?"

"I was going to use my friend's hunting guns at his place," Daniel said in a matter-of-fact tone.

Needless to say, this terrified me! Daniel had tried to kill himself when he was thirteen; he had felt that committing suicide would bring him to his birth father. After a time of therapy,

I thought Daniel had rejected the suicide option; I assumed we were past this. The doctor was also alarmed and immediately sent us to the emergency room, where we waited hours for Daniel to be admitted to an adult mental-health facility. Two weeks later, he convinced the therapists that he was no longer a danger to himself, and we brought him home.

After taking antidepressant medication, Daniel seemed to be more like his normal self, the guy who wanted to talk about cars constantly, the son who would bake apple crisp for the family and say, "Mom, how about if I make you some hot chocolate?"

But as soon as he began feeling better, Daniel decided he no longer needed the pills. I counted the pills in his bottle and knew he was ignoring our advice to keep taking the medication, so we pleaded with him to continue.

We met with his psychiatrist, who agreed that he could go off the medication. Daniel's outlook had certainly improved, but Jeff and I were still worried he might fall back into depression. Yet the dark Midwest winter was over, and the spring sunshine was likely helping him, so we told ourselves he simply could be prone to seasonal affective disorder, a common problem in northern Wisconsin. And at least he had agreed to keep seeing a therapist.

The fall after Daniel graduated from high school in 2012 and turned twenty, he started technical college. I thought he would flourish there since he was interested in the courses. But his adjustment was difficult.

"These classes are too hard," he'd say. "I don't think I can do them."

"You just started," we told him. "Give it a chance. Don't give up so fast."

Soon he was staying out all night, "hanging out with friends," and we had to remind him that while he still lived at home, we expected to know where he was.

LIVING IN DENIAL

We were naive parents. We hadn't realized he was drinking and doing drugs. It's so easy to believe the best about your kid. Believing the worst and being suspicious didn't come naturally to me. When I found a bong on his bed and he said he was only holding on to it as a favor for a friend and didn't use it, I thought it must be true. We destroyed the bong, but I'm still amazed at what had to be my denial of something staring me right in the face!

Daniel had always been a risk taker. I was always telling him to stop doing flips off the end of the dock so he wouldn't break his neck. Impulsive behavior came easy to him; considering consequences did not. But now his risk taking was becoming extremely dangerous.

We faced reality that fall as my husband answered a middle-of-the-night phone call.

"Yes," I heard my husband saying. "I'll be there as soon as I can."

It was the sheriff's department in the next county. Daniel had been arrested for drinking and driving. By the time my husband brought home a drunk and belligerent Daniel, my shock had turned to anger.

"You could have killed someone! And how can you drink vodka? You saw what it did to your mother!"

"Vodka is in my genes," he said.

With the ugliness of hostility covering his face, he turned away and walked out the door.

RIDING AN EMOTIONAL ROLLER COASTER

Jeff and I found ourselves riding a roller coaster of emotions—hopeful one day, frustrated and fearful the next as Daniel would make promises but not keep them. He began to be agitated around us and detached. This wasn't the Daniel we knew; we didn't like this kid! He even started lying to Masha.

We held back our frustration as he ignored our advice and made one bad choice after another. We needed to remain calm and keep showing him love because we were trying to persuade him to enter treatment. He was no longer a minor, and we couldn't force him into a program.

When Daniel said he wanted to quit college, we were supportive. Maybe a job would be the key to his recovery; maybe he would gain confidence and purpose again. He had been a lifeguard in high school and had always been responsible on the job.

And then the roller coaster took a terrifying drop. The track beneath us simply disappeared. Jeff and I discovered he'd been stealing money and my credit card from my purse. I felt all the blood drain from my face. It was as if I had no blood at all—I was a wax dummy, devoid of life. At first my thoughts were shallow, superficial, because deeper thoughts were too frightening.

Ah. Now I understand. I didn't keep misplacing my card or just imagine I'd had another twenty-dollar bill in my purse. I'm not going crazy—my son stole it. Just as he stole a check and tried to cash it at our bank.

It didn't take long for the complicated mix of emotions that had overwhelmed our family life for months to intensify. I felt like an idiot. How could we have let this happen? I felt angry and hurt. Jeff and I felt betrayed—the credit-card history showed he had used my card at a certain gas station for a year. When my husband paid the bill, he thought I was simply filling up the car.

Daniel promised not to steal anymore; he cried and apologized profusely. He said all the right words in the right way. The very next week, he stole my card again. This time we felt numb. We were growing weary of the roller coaster ride. Wasn't it time to climb off? We couldn't trust Daniel in our home any longer; he had even stolen things from Masha.

Daniel moved in with friends, but we eventually got him a

spot in a Salvation Army shelter where he was forced to attend Alcoholics Anonymous meetings and talk regularly with a Salvation Army life coach. The shelter even set him up with a job at the factory across the street. Again, we hoped and prayed for the best, for a turnaround, for a miracle from God.

Then once again, the roller coaster plunged from hope to despair when he was fired from the job and kicked out of the shelter for breaking the rules and doing drugs. Besides marijuana, he had added methamphetamine to the alcohol.

One Friday Jeff and I rushed home from work after Masha had called me, crying.

"A deputy's here, and he has a gun," she'd told me in a panic.

"What?"

"He thinks I know who broke into the house next door, but I don't know!"

"Honey, I'm on my way home. I'm staying on the phone with you until I get there."

I drove up to see a sheriff's deputy—wearing a bulletproof vest and carrying a gun—standing next to my daughter on our front porch. Like a mama bear protecting her cub, I marched up to the officer and demanded to know why he hadn't called us instead of intimidating our daughter. I didn't get a satisfactory answer, but we learned that someone had broken into the empty house next door and had been living there. Someone was in there now, and the deputies thought he was dangerous.

The nightmare continued as we crowded around a window inside our home, watching officers with guns and dogs circle the house as one officer lifted a bullhorn to his mouth.

"Come out with your hands up," he shouted, just like they do in the movies.

That's it, I thought. *We're in some horrible movie. This really isn't happening.*

The scene felt surreal—and yet it wasn't. Masha, Jeff, and I prayed together, asking God to keep the officers and the person in the house safe.

Then we said what we feared in our hearts: "Lord, please don't let it be Daniel!"

The horror show continued as we watched a tall, young man exit the house.

As we watched deputies throw him to the ground and hand-cuff him.

As we realized the young man was indeed Daniel.

I still remember the deputy standing in our doorway, telling us they had hoped to find two other men, the ones who broke into the place with our son. They were taking Daniel to the county jail, where he would be incarcerated until court on Monday. Did we want to post bail?

We didn't. We thought the experience of spending two nights in jail might be a wake-up call for Daniel. And to tell you the truth, we were relieved to have him there. A church friend was working at the jail that weekend and talked with Daniel, trying to help him get back on the right path. We kept hoping and praying that this was Daniel's rock bottom. Maybe this would make a difference.

But nothing changed. I'm not even sure what I was feeling then. Those days were a blur of despair and prayers, of exhaustion and mounting numbness. How could we help our son when he didn't even want our help? In the movie *A River Runs Through It*, Rev. Maclean expresses the helplessness I felt at the time:

> Each one of us here today will at one time in our lives
> look upon a loved one who is in need and ask the
> same question: We are willing help, Lord, but what, if
> anything, is needed? . . . Either we don't know what part

of ourselves to give or, more often than not, the part
we have to give is not wanted. And so it is those we live
with and should know who elude us. But we can still
love them—we can love completely without complete
understanding.[1]

TRYING TO INTERVENE

After Daniel ended up living in a trailer home with other meth
users, I was desperate to take any action I could. So I wrote a
two-page intervention letter to him, as a drug treatment center
had recommended. In it I reminded him of his good qualities,
but also of how addiction had stolen those qualities from him.
It was an illness that needed treatment, just like cancer. I wrote
painstakingly, avoiding the English cursive writing he had never
learned and couldn't read.

And then I drove to the trailer to deliver it and convince him
to come home with me. I was a bit fearful. I didn't know who
else was inside the trailer, and I was alone. Still, nothing could
have stopped me. I had to do everything within my power to grab
hold of my son's heart.

Daniel was angry with me when I gave him the letter. He
yelled and threw it in the air. My words, trapped in the envelope,
settled on the floor of the trailer's porch:

> *I love you, Daniel, and so do Dad and Masha, but we
> would like to see you get healthy. We knew you before, when
> you didn't lie or steal. You can beat this addiction and learn
> to be happy in a healthy way! But you will need to make
> a decision. If you do, we will help you. Masha needs her
> brother. We need our son back. God has plans for you! All
> you have to do is take the first step. Progress, not perfection!
> You can have a good life!*

After he slammed the door of the trailer home behind him, I picked up the letter and tucked it inside the screen door. I wasn't sure if he would ever read it. Feeling weary and heartbroken, I climbed back into the car and sat there for a moment. What else could I do?

CHOOSING THE WILDERNESS

One day Daniel showed up at my door on a Monday, a day when I just happened to be working from home. He told me he'd been to church the day before with a friend who was trying to help him.

"At church, God told me He could lead me out of the wilderness," Daniel said, yet his face looked tormented. His drug-addicted friends were in the car waiting for him, but I sensed my son wanted to stay with me. He hugged me for the longest time.

"You don't want to go, do you?" I said.

"No," he answered. But he didn't step away from the doorway.

"Then stay here!" I urged. If I could have wrestled this tall, young man to the ground to keep him with me, I would have. "Ask God to lead you out of the wilderness. We'll figure something out. We'll help you."

In the end, the pull of addiction was too much for him, and he left. I watched the car go down our driveway and prayed that God would save our Daniel from the lions' den.

OUR GREATEST FEAR

And then on September 30, 2013, not long after his twenty-first birthday, the tragedy we feared most happened: Daniel shot and killed himself.

As I write these words three and a half years later, I can still feel the complete and utter shock I felt as I saw the sorrow in my husband's eyes and heard him tell me Daniel was dead. I still hear myself screaming. I feel myself dropping to the floor and pounding my fists into the carpet, sobbing uncontrollably. I see the image of Daniel's embalmed body—a towel covering his head—and feel his cold hands in mine.

This was not the happy ending of my prayers. I was praying for his complete healing, an earthly deliverance, and it didn't come. I was waiting to see how God would use all of Daniel's pain for the good of others. I was expecting Daniel to visit me in the nursing home when I was old and talk my ear off as he usually did. He was supposed to fix our cars and feed me rice pudding in my old age. That was our joke. Now who would feed me when I was old, blind, and toothless?

Daniel was kind enough to write a good-bye note, even though this part of his letter seemed cruelly ironic to us:

You tried raising me to become a successful young man even with my addictions and struggles, and you did everything I could ever ask for. You took on the role of parents, and I couldn't be happier for that. I love you guys and always will, and I'll never forget what you've done for me.

It was ironic because we felt we had failed him—and in the worst way, with no more second chances.

The heavy grief, sorrow, and guilt immobilized me. I was crushed by the weight of my inability to save my son's life, as if it were all in my mortal hands. My grief and guilt were interrupted only by anger. Ten years after adopting him and loving him, praying for him and caring for him, he was suddenly gone—this boy whom God specifically chose to place in our home, this boy I'd loved with all my heart! It made no sense to me.

Dr. Julianna Slattery notes that God gives parents "great influence" over their children, but "no *control*."[2] For parents, that truth can be hard to accept.

One adoptive father says, "I'm convinced we are not responsible for the outcome of the lives of the children God places in our path. We are simply called to love them in the best way we know how."[3]

Yet it was so very easy for my husband and me to think the best way we knew how wasn't good enough. We'd been given Daniel's belongings, the few items he had with him when he died. My intervention letter was there—folded and wrinkled. He had read it; it had meant something to him. What if I had written another letter or done something—anything—else? What if we had talked to him the day he decided to end his life? The fact that we didn't devastated us.

Right before Daniel's funeral, my friend Michael Furchert sent me an email presenting an eternal perspective that may be a good reminder for all of us who struggle with helping our children heal:

> *I cannot begin to imagine the many questions you must have in your mind at this heart-wrenching time. And the questions you might have toward your heavenly Father— why, after all you have given and gone through, you now have to bear this as well? Why did Daniel's life and your calling to take him into your home and family have to end like this? We might never know.*
>
> *I am certain, however, that God always knew about the brevity of Daniel's life, and that He led you toward him so that Daniel would know that he was loved. He led you toward him so that many years would be added to his burdened life through the care and compassion he encountered in your home and family. And He led you toward him so that Daniel would meet Christ and through you be adopted into God's family as well, so that despite the*

*sorrow that would one day wear him down, he would be
saved and justified through your faith and witness.*

*And as tragic as this story might now have ended,
you have in the end saved his life through what God had
chosen you to do, as you have placed Daniel's life and soul
at the foot of the cross so many times. Maybe this was the
most important and most difficult mission and ministry
any human could be asked to do. And you have done it
faithfully with all the strength you had for as long as God
gave you the opportunity to do so.*

*Difficult days will still be ahead as you learn to come
to terms with this. You might struggle with yourself,
wondering if there was more you could have done, if you
missed something, if you could have prevented it. Maybe,
Julie, your most important calling wasn't to save his life but
to spare his soul! So much in life is outside of our control,
especially as we see and witness the struggle of others. We
can only reach out to them, embrace and love them, laugh
and cry with them, and show them Christ.*

*You will forever miss Daniel. But what you have done
for him will carry on into eternity—and there you will
meet him again. And he will know that it is because of all
that you have done for him that he is there in the presence
of the One who through you, Jeff, and your family became
his heavenly Father.*

THE BEST GOTCHA DAY

While my faith told me Daniel was in heaven, and my brain
told me he no longer suffered from his inner turmoil, my soul
continued to grieve, and my body couldn't move.

A friend of mine was praying and wishing she could do more
for me when Jesus assured her that He was interceding for me.

And I could feel that He was. He showered me with comfort and care and miraculously lifted the heaviest weight of my grief so I was able to move my legs, leave my bed, and function. But a sense of peace was missing.

Eight months later, June 2, 2014, arrived, the anniversary of the day Daniel and Masha officially became Holmquists in a Russian courtroom. We call that day Gotcha Day—as in "We gotcha!" In 2004 we had walked out the courthouse door and into the sunny June day as an official family. Jeff snapped a few photos, and then it was time to celebrate. I still remember the joy of our Russian tea shop lunch that followed, our delight as we ate our treats and bought bundles of sweet-smelling lilies of the valley from a little salesgirl. We were giddy as we left Bryansk in the van filled with supplies of toilet paper for the orphanage, laughing as the packages toppled onto our heads with every bump in the road.

For the next nine years, our family celebrated Gotcha Day on June 2 with a restaurant dinner and an enormous bonfire. Each year after Christmas, we dragged our pine tree out of the living room and into our large yard, where it would grow dry and brittle. On June 2, the tree put on a dramatic show in our bonfire pit, its flames leaping twenty feet high in a red blaze of glory. We'd watch the sparks fly against the darkness of the summer evening and roast marshmallows on the remaining embers, all the while remembering how God had brought us together.

But our first Gotcha Day without Daniel wasn't something we wanted to face. Jeff and I prayed specifically for Masha that morning, asking God to send His comfort to this girl who had lost so much. Then I drove to work.

A little while later, Anna, who was by then an adult living on her own, sent us this email:

I wanted to tell you that after I woke up this morning, I fell back asleep. And I had this dream. There was a big party, and Daniel was there, and he was smiling and dancing. It was definitely his party. I went over to him and hugged him and told him I missed him. He told me it was okay, and that he was happy. And we just chatted for a while. He was having a great time dancing and singing with all of these people who were celebrating him, and he was happy to see me. He sends his love to all of you. Then I woke up. Just wanted to share, especially after I realized that today is Gotcha Day. Don't worry—they didn't forget about the holiday up there.

With this one short email, God gave me peace and allowed me to taste the joy Daniel was experiencing. For my heart suddenly realized that my Russian son was now celebrating the ultimate Gotcha Day with his eternal Father. As an adopted child of God, every day is now a glorious Gotcha Day celebration for Daniel.

Now when I read Hebrews 12:22, I can see my son among the happy throng of angels and saints gone before: "You have come to Mount Zion, to the city of the living God, the heavenly Jerusalem. You have come to thousands upon thousands of angels in joyful assembly" (NIV).

SOMETHING BEAUTIFUL

There was another balm for our wound of grief following Daniel's death. Long before Daniel's life spiraled out of control, one of his former girlfriends had tried overdosing on pills. Here's what she wrote to me about that time:

I had to stay in the hospital overnight, and [Daniel] kept checking on me. And when I came home the next day, he

was waiting at my house for me. He stayed late and just
simply hung out with me to make sure I was okay. You know
how his goofiness was—he lit up every room. He just kept
encouraging me and just always made me feel loved. When
we lost him, my world crashed again. I didn't understand
why he got to go and I didn't. Then with your help, I found
God. I realized I can't give up. Daniel wouldn't want me to.
I know that my time isn't done here, and that I need to keep
helping people that suffer like he did.

It helps a grieving heart to see life where there was only sorrow, to see God redeem something tragic by saving another soul.
Don't we long to see God bring beauty from ashes?

As I was writing this last chapter, I happened to find my old
journal and an entry written two weeks after Daniel's death:

God says He will make something beautiful from the
broken pieces of Daniel's life, from his broken death, and
from our broken lives. So I have to trust Him, even though
I don't know what that could possibly mean.

I believe that "something beautiful" includes my message to
you: Adopting Daniel was more than worth it, and I'd do it all
over again. Even though we lost our son, adopting him, loving
him, and learning from him was worth the pain involved. Our
momentary suffering was a small price to pay for Daniel's eternal
life with his heavenly Father.

Awhile back, I was able to see Daniel's good friend Jonny. He's
tall like Daniel was, and when I reached up to hug him good-bye,
I felt my Russian boy's embrace. I miss Daniel's generous shows
of affection and caring. But someday in heaven, he'll wrap his
arms around me once more.

Masha was with me as we talked to Jonny, and I know the

hug she received from him comforted her, too. God helped her through that dark period, and she's now a stable and independent young woman who loves and appreciates her family.

A CHANGED LIFE

Like Daniel, Hannah Johnson had thoughts of ending her life and had tried to harm herself numerous times. She grew up being abused and living around alcoholism, but when she was fifteen, Jeff and Jessamy Johnson adopted her. The adoption was definitely worth it; their relationship changed Hannah's life.

"I don't even know where I'd be right now if I didn't get adopted," Hannah says. "Mom and Dad kept telling me that they wouldn't give up on me, that there was nothing I could do to cause that, but a part of me didn't believe it. Sometimes I would put them to the test to prove that what they said was actually true.

"It's easy to feel like people will give up on you, that you're worthless, that you don't deserve a good family. It's just easy for me to feel that way. But they never gave up on me—not once."

As Hannah lived with her new parents and attended church with them, she began to see evidence that God was real. Yet she was behind academically and struggling in school. She needed a setting that would better fit her academic, emotional, and spiritual needs. The family eventually discovered Evangelhouse Christian Academy for girls, a clinically driven, therapeutic boarding school located in a different state.

Hannah and her parents were sure that God had chosen the school. But then the Johnsons looked at the cost—ten thousand dollars *per month*. The couple didn't have that kind of money. They moved forward regardless, ready to sell their house to pay the tuition. Hannah has now attended the school for more than a year and a half, and God has provided the money each month. The Johnsons didn't even need to sell their home.

"I know this is all according to God's plan," says Hannah, who is now eighteen. "I really feel that He knew this was the best place for me. It's changed me so much, and I feel that can only come from God. I'm also happy that my parents have done so much for me. Our relationship has grown so much together."

For any of us wondering why a young person can think of ending his or her life, Hannah offers important insight:

> Sometimes you feel like the only way you can deal with the past is to hurt yourself and to end your own life. But I've learned that life can feel really hard—like you want to give up—and that this happens to everybody. But there's hope. When you know God you don't have to give up.
>
> I realize now that I might be feeling a certain way, but I'm not always going to feel like that. So I need to find coping skills that will give me more hope, whether it's listing positive things about my life, or listing what I love about myself, or praying.

A few short years ago, Hannah's life revolved around emotional chaos and self-destruction. Now it revolves around God and healing.

"I'm very passionate about giving my life to Him," Hannah explains. "I know that the only way I can truly get better is to have Him in my life, as the center of everything."

She only wishes other foster children would have the same chance to heal. "Everybody deserves parents," she says. "If you don't have any, the greatest thing anybody could do is take you as their own. I have a lot of friends who haven't been adopted. They say they don't even know what to do with their lives, and a lot of them are out on the streets. They didn't get to have the privilege that I did, and I wish that they did."

BE A REBUILDER

Although the stories of Hannah and Daniel are as different as two stories can be, both show Christian parents doing their best to lift children out of the rubble of life and a destructive past so they can point them toward Jesus. Adoption cannot exist without a child's loss. As adoptive parents, we're called to help rebuild after that loss, with the hope that we will one day see our children resting firmly on the foundation of God.

Consider again with me the Israelites who rebuilt the house of the Lord after the Babylonian captivity. The people of Judah had been hauled to Babylon decades earlier, and Jerusalem had been completely destroyed. But when the time was right, God stirred the heart of Cyrus, king of Persia, and he allowed the Jews to return to their city.

Not all the exiled Jews left Babylon to return to Jerusalem and rebuild the temple. The trip would take four months; they would have to trek across nine hundred miles of dangerous land where bandits roamed. Some of the exiles were too old to make the trip; others chose not to go but donated resources. Still others no doubt decided to stay in Babylon, which probably seemed safer than that perilous journey. After all, Babylon was a rather comfortable exile for the Jews: They had synagogues, and many were scholars; they could even become wealthy there. Of the two to three million Jewish exiles, only fifty thousand chose to return to Judah.

Who were these people? "Everyone whose spirit God had stirred" (Ezra 1:5); "everyone whose heart God had moved" (NIV). They chose to follow God's call despite the risk.

It wasn't easy rebuilding Jerusalem and the temple, but those Jews stayed faithful to their calling. The sacrifices of these rebuilders were great, but they proved worthwhile as they saw their homeland come to life once more.

Is God calling you to be a rebuilder? Has He called you to help restore the heart of a child, a heart that is now crumbling, a heart that needs to know God?

Make no mistake, no matter where your journey takes you, no matter the pain and trials you may encounter, this call will be worthwhile. The Father who adopted you will walk with you on the way, reminding you that He is pleased with you, equipping you with His provision, building your faith, showing His heart to you, sharing with you His deep love for orphans—and you.

Rest Stop

Has God moved your heart and stirred your soul, asking you to answer a call to love and begin a journey toward adoption? If He has, ask Him to help you take the next step on the road. Record your conversation on your journal page.

My Journey to Adoption

DATE _____

I rescued the poor who cried for help, and the
fatherless who had none to assist them.

Job 29:12, NIV

Acknowledgments

To my husband, Jeff, for always supporting my dreams and God's calling upon my life; for cleaning, cooking, and doing without his companion weekend after weekend as I wrote; for providing the first critique and edit; for being willing to share his life in this book; and for being a calm, patient, and loving father with a servant's heart.

To my children, Anna, Ben, and Masha, for supporting this book 100 percent.

To the parents who shared their stories and their hearts with me, thank you for trusting me and allowing me the privilege of entering into your lives. You are my heroes!

To my supporters at Focus on the Family, Larry Weeden and Kelly Rosati, for backing my proposal and making this book possible; and to Liz Duckworth, for her encouragement and editorial expertise; and to Jennifer Lonas, my fabulous copyeditor.

To my friend and adoptive mom, Sue Eitemiller, for her insightful critique of my manuscript, especially the last chapter.

To my parents, Esther and Vernon Buscho, who helped us financially to welcome Daniel and Masha into our lives and to say good-bye to Daniel. I'm so blessed to have such generous and supportive parents! Thanks for always being there for me and my family.

Appendix: Resources

COUNSELING

Focus on the Family Counseling Services and Referrals—Focus on the Family
has licensed professional counselors who are available to listen, pray, and
provide guidance. You can arrange to speak with a counselor at no cost
by calling 1-855-771-HELP (4357) Monday through Friday between 6:00
a.m. and 8:00 p.m. Mountain Standard Time.

WEBSITES

Association for Training on Trauma and Attachment in Children (ATTACH)—
includes a list of qualified attachment counselors by state; 310 E. 38th Street,
Suite 320, Minneapolis, MN 55409; 612-861-4222; attach.org.

Christian Alliance for Orphans (CAFO)—offers monthly webinars, links
to adoption resources and organizations, audio recordings from past
conferences, and more; 6723 Whittier Avenue, Suite 202, McLean, VA 22101;
cafo.org.

Empowered to Connect—adoptive parenting resource library of articles, audios,
and videos; empoweredtoconnect.org.

Karyn Purvis Institute of Child Development—a program of Texas Christian
University offering research, education, intervention training, and outreach
to improve outcomes for children who have experienced trauma; TCU Box
298921, Fort Worth, TX 76129; 817-257-7415; child.tcu.edu.

CONFERENCES

Christian Alliance for Orphans Summit (CAFO Summit)—annual conference
designed to inspire and equip Christians "to care for orphans with wisdom-
guided love"; cafo.org/summit.

Empowered to Connect Conference—"two-day conference designed to
help adoptive and foster parents, ministry leaders and professionals

better understand how to connect with 'children from hard places' in order to help them heal and become all that God desires them to be"; empoweredtoconnect.org/conferences.

Refresh Conference—an annual conference in a few locations across the country. The conference offers adoptive and foster parents worship, fellowship, teaching, and expert training; Overlake Christian Church, 9900 Willows Road NE, Redmond, WA 98052; refresh@occ.org; refreshgatherings.org.

Notes

CHAPTER 1—GREAT EXPECTATIONS

1. Kimberley Raunikar Taylor, *The Intentional Family: Celebrating Adoption* (Kansas City: Beacon Hill Press, 2007), 102.
2. Ibid., 122.
3. Sharon Kaplan Roszia, from the foreword to *Wounded Children, Healing Homes: How Traumatized Children Impact Adoptive and Foster Families,* by Jayne E. Schooler, Betsy Keefer Smalley, Timothy J. Callahan (Colorado Springs: NavPress, 2009), 7, 8.
4. "Francis Chan – It's Not about You," YouTube video, 3:42, from a sermon posted by Preacher Talks, October 6, 2015, https://www.youtube.com /watch?v=U_MK8uDz4nU.

CHAPTER 2—REALITY SHOW: INFERTILITY

1. Laura Bush, *Spoken from the Heart* (New York: Scribner, 2010), 104.
2. Sheridan Voysey, *Resurrection Year: Turning Broken Dreams into New Beginnings* (Nashville: Thomas Nelson, 2013), 20.
3. Josh Lindstrom, "Joy and Gladness," part 1 of "Good News, Great Joy" series (sermon, Woodmen Valley Chapel, Colorado Springs, Colorado, November 30, 2014).
4. Philip Yancey, September 2007 *Open House* interview by Sheridan Voysey, quoted in Voysey, *Resurrection Year*, 43.
5. Russell D. Moore, *Adopted for Life: The Priority of Adoption for Christian Families and Churches* (Wheaton, IL: Crossway, 2009), 101.
6. Dr. Karyn Purvis, broadcast interview by Jim Daly, "Connecting with Your Child (Part 2 of 2)," *Focus on the Family*, May 20, 2016.
7. Ann Kiemel Anderson, quoted in "A Focus on the Family Friend Has Gone Home," *Daly Focus* (blog), Focus on the Family, March 4, 2014, http://jimdaly .focusonthefamily.com/a-focus-on-the-family-friend-has-gone-home/.
8. David Platt, *Counter Culture: Following Christ in an Anti-Christian Age* (Carol Stream, IL: Tyndale, 2017), 82.
9. Ibid., 82–83.

CHAPTER 3—REALITY SHOW: WOUNDED CHILDREN

1. Data from Jo Jones and Paul Placek, *Adoption by the Numbers: A Comprehensive Report of U.S. Adoption Statistics*, eds. Chuck Johnson and Megan Lestino (Alexandria, VA: National Council For Adoption, 2017), ii.
2. Ibid., 30.
3. Ibid., 10.
4. *The AFCARS Report*, No. 22, US Department of Health and Human Services, Administration for Children and Families, Administration on Children, Youth and Families, Children's Bureau, https://www.acf.hhs.gov/sites/default/files/cb/afcarsreport22.pdf.
5. Jedd Medefind, *Becoming Home* (Grand Rapids: Zondervan, 2013), e-book.
6. Kathy Ledesma, interview by Jeff Nelson in "Sandra Bullock's Adoption: A Foster Care Expert Answers the Big Questions," *People*, December 2, 2015.
7. P. J. Pecora et al., "Mental Health of Current and Former Recipients of Foster Care: A Review of Recent Studies in the USA," *Child and Family Social Work* 14, no. 2 (May 2009): 132–46.
8. Dr. Karyn Purvis, broadcast interview by Jim Daly, "Connecting with Your Child (Part 2 of 2)," *Focus on the Family*, May 20, 2016.
9. Daniel J. Bennett, *A Passion for the Fatherless: Developing a God-Centered Ministry to Orphans* (Grand Rapids: Kregel, 2011), 104.
10. Deborah N. Silverstein and Sharon Kaplan, "Lifelong Issues in Adoption," 1982, http://www.fairfamilies.org/2012/1999/99LifelongIssues.htm.
11. Child Welfare Information Gateway, accessed July 28, 2017, www.childwelfare.gov/topics/adoption/intro/issues/.
12. Silverstein and Kaplan, "Lifelong Issues in Adoption."
13. Purvis, broadcast interview by Jim Daly (Part 1 of 2), May 19, 2016.
14. Bessel A. van der Kolk and Christine A. Courtois, "Editorial comments: Complex developmental trauma," *Journal of Traumatic Stress* 18 (2005): 385–88.
15. Debi Grebenik, "Traits of Successful Adoptive Families," Focus on the Family, accessed January 1, 2016, www.focusonthefamily.com/parenting/adoptive-families/traits-of-successful-adoptive-families/characteristics-of-successful-adoptive-families.
16. Diana Stone, "Why Doesn't God Answer My Prayers?," *Today's Christian Woman*, June 24, 2015.

CHAPTER 4—FACING FEAR

1. Susan J. Astley et al., "Application of the Fetal Alcohol Syndrome Facial Photographic Screening Tool in a Foster Care Population," *Journal of Pediatrics* 141, no. 5 (November 2002): 712–17, www.ncbi.nlm.nih.gov/pubmed/12410204, cited in "FASD Basics for Foster Parents."
2. Robin Chernoff et al., "Assessing the Health Status of Children Entering Foster Care," *Pediatrics* 93, no. 4 (April 1994): 594–601, www.ncbi.nlm.nih.gov/pubmed/8134214, cited in "FASD Basics for Foster Parents."

3. "Why Kids Don't 'Outgrow' Reactive Attachment Disorder (and What Happens When They Grow Up without Help)," Institute for Attachment and Child Development, February 8, 2017, http://instituteforattachment .ong/why-kids-dont-outgrow-reactive-attachment-disorder-and-what -happens-when-they-grow-up-without-help/.

4. Ibid.

CHAPTER 5—LISTENING TO GOD

1. Irene Garcia with Lissa Halls Johnson, *Rich in Love: When God Rescues Messy People* (Colorado Springs: David C Cook, 2014), 90.

2. Julie Holmquist, "No More Waiting," *Thriving Family*, October/November 2014, 26–27.

CHAPTER 6—GATHERING SUPPORT

1. John and Tricia Goyer, broadcast interview by Jim Daly, "Making Room in Your Life for a Child in Need," *Focus on the Family*, May 9, 2016.

2. Adapted and paraphrased from Julie Holmquist, "Adoptive Families Need Help," *Thriving Family*, February/March 2015.

3. Ibid.

CHAPTER 7—WAITING

1. Kathy Ledesma, "Adopting from Foster Care," *Adoptive Families*, accessed April 17, 2017, www.adoptivefamilies.com/how-to-adopt/foster-care -adoption/adopting-from-foster-care/.

2. Kimberley Raunikar Taylor, *The Intentional Family: Celebrating Adoption* (Kansas City: Beacon Hill Press, 2007), 69.

3. Ibid.

4. John and Tricia Goyer, broadcast interview by Jim Daly, "Making Room in Your Life for a Child in Need," *Focus on the Family*, May 9, 2016.

5. Russell Kelfer, "Wait," http://dtm.org/life-lessons/read/selected-poems-by -russell-(readprint).

CHAPTER 8—BUILDING FAITH

1. Mary Beth Chapman with Ellen Vaughn, *Choosing to See: A Journey of Struggle and Hope* (Grand Rapids: Revell, 2010), 86.

2. Ibid., 86, 87, 88.

CHAPTER 9—FOSTER-CARE CHALLENGES

1. D. J. Jordan, comments at Evangelicals for Life Conference, Washington, DC, 2017.

2. Rosaria Champagne Butterfield, *The Secret Thoughts of an Unlikely Convert: An English Professor's Journey into Christian Faith* (Pittsburgh: Crown and Covenant, 2015), 123.

3. Ibid., 130.

4. Matthew Henry, *Commentary on the Whole Bible*, vol. 6, *Acts to Revelation*, s.v. "Hebrews," chap. 11, sec. 4.2, Christian Classics Ethereal Library, www .ccel.org/ccel/henry/mhc6.Heb.xii.html.

5. Charles Spurgeon, *Morning and Evening* (New Kensington, PA: Whitaker House, 2001), 574.

CHAPTER 10—LOVING LIKE JESUS

1. *Refreshing Words: 40 Days of Renewal for Foster and Adoptive Parents* (Redmond, WA: Refresh Conference, 2015), 77.

2. Linda Folden Palmer, *The Baby Bond: The New Science Behind What's Really Important When Caring for Your Baby* (Naperville, IL: Sourcebooks, 2009), 40.

3. Irene Garcia with Lissa Halls Johnson, *Rich in Love: When God Rescues Messy People* (Colorado Springs: David C Cook, 2014), 117–18.

4. John and Tricia Goyer, broadcast interview by Jim Daly, "Making Room in Your Life for a Child in Need," *Focus on the Family*, May 9, 2016.

CHAPTER 11—JOY AND GRIEF

1. Adapted from Debbie Riley with John Meeks, *Beneath the Mask: Understanding Adopted Teens* (Silver Spring, MD: C.A.S.E., 2005), 90.

2. C. S. Lewis, *A Grief Observed* (New York: HarperOne, 1961), 60.

3. Tara Vanderwoude, "Quotable Adoption Phrases?" October 22, 2014, taravanderwoude.com/thoughts, http://www.taravanderwoude.com/?offset =1425322944511.

4. Christina Romo, "An Adoptee's Perspective," *Adoption Today* (special edition) 15, no. 5 (2013): 8.

CHAPTER 12—A DEEPER TRUST

1. David L. Chandler, "How Spider Webs Achieve Their Strength," MIT News, February 2, 2012, http://news.mit.edu/2012/spider-web-strength-0202.

2. Ibid.

3. Maris Blechner, "Inducement: Adoption Language We Must Understand," North American Council on Adoptable Children, February 9, 2004, https:// www.nacac.org/resource/inducement-adoption-language/.

4. Adapted and paraphrased from Julie Holmquist, "Winning Our Son's Trust," *Adoptive Families*, March 2008.

5. Matthew Henry, *Commentary on the Whole Bible*, vol. 6, *Acts to Revelation*, s.v. "Hebrews," chap. 6, sec. 4.3.3, Christian Classics Ethereal Library, http://www.ccel.org/ccel/henry/mhc6.Heb.vii.html.

6. Ernie Johnson, *Unscripted: The Unpredictable Moments That Make Life Extraordinary* (Grand Rapids: Baker Books, 2017), 199.

7. Ibid.

8. Ann Spangler, *Praying the Names of God: A Daily Guide* (Grand Rapids: Zondervan, 2004), 267.

CHAPTER 13—SPIRITUAL BATTLES

1. Shelly Radic, quoted in Julie Holmquist, "Adoptive Families Need Help," *Thriving Family*, February/March 2015.
2. Brian Borgman, *After They Are Yours: The Grace and Grit of Adoption* (Minneapolis: Cruciform Press, 2014), 56.
3. Mary E. DeMuth, *Beautiful Battle: A Woman's Guide to Spiritual Warfare* (Eugene, OR: Harvest House, 2012), 14, 15.
4. Borgman, *After They Are Yours*, 78–79.
5. John Bevere, *The Bait of Satan: Living Free from the Deadly Trap of Offense* (Lake Mary, FL: Charisma House, 2014), 9–10.
6. Ibid., 11.
7. Borgman, *After They Are Yours*, 56.

CHAPTER 15—FORGIVENESS

1. R. T. Kendall, *Total Forgiveness* (Lake Mary, FL: Charisma House, 2007), 176–77.
2. Brandy Lee, "When I Didn't Love My Adopted Child," *Christianity Today*, March 2016, www.christianitytoday.com/women/2016/march/when-i-didnt-love-my-adopted-child.html.
3. John R. W. Stott, ed., *The Message of the Sermon on the Mount* (Downers Grove, IL: InterVarsity Press, 1978), 40–42.
4. Jerry Bridges, *The Blessing of Humility* (Colorado Springs: NavPress, 2016), 23.
5. Timothy Keller, *Walking with God through Pain and Suffering* (New York: Riverhead Books, 2013), 228.
6. Jim Elliot, *The Journals of Jim Elliot*, ed. Elisabeth Elliot (Grand Rapids: Revell, 1978), 125–26.
7. Corrie ten Boom, "I'm Still Learning to Forgive," *Guideposts*, November 1972, 3.

CHAPTER 16—THE HEALING PATH

1. Dr. Karyn Purvis, broadcast interview by Jim Daly, "Connecting with Your Child (Part 1 of 2)," *Focus on the Family*, May 19, 2016.
2. Robert W. Kellemen, PhD, *God's Healing for Life's Losses: How to Find Hope When You're Hurting* (Winona Lake, IN: BMH Books, 2010), 53.

CHAPTER 17—WORTH THE RISK

1. *A River Runs Through It*, directed by Robert Redford (Allied Filmmakers/Columbia Pictures, 1992).
2. Julianna Slattery, *Guilt-Free Motherhood: Parenting with Godly Wisdom* (Deerfield Beach, FL: Faith Communications, 2004), 169, emphasis added.
3. *Refreshing Words: 40 Days of Renewal for Foster and Adoptive Parents* (Redmond, WA: Refresh Conference, 2015), 77.

About the Author

Julie Holmquist accepted Jesus Christ as her Savior at age fourteen but didn't surrender her life to Him until she was thirty-four. At that time, God gave her a passion to write for Him, and she started by publishing testimonies in the two community newspapers she owned with her husband, Jeff, and then later in a blog that received recognition from the Evangelical Press Association.

A former award-winning journalist and communications director with a bachelor's degree in German and journalism, Julie now works as a book editor at Focus on the Family in Colorado Springs, Colorado. She and Jeff have been married for more than thirty years and worked together for eleven years as newspaper publishers in Osceola, Wisconsin, where they raised their four children. Julie enjoys hiking in the beauty of God's nature, traveling, learning more about God's Word, and encouraging others. Contact her at JulieHolmquist.com or by email at jholmquistmedia@gmail.com.

Inspiring Books to Guide Your Journey of Adoption

AVAILABLE AT FINE RETAILERS EVERYWHERE AND AT

WWW.FOCUSONTHEFAMILY.COM/RESOURCES

THE KINGDOM SERIES FROM DR. TONY EVANS

MORE RESOURCES TO GROW YOUR FAITH AND FURTHER GOD'S KINGDOM!

KINGDOM MAN
978-1-58997-685-6

KINGDOM MAN
DEVOTIONAL
978-1-62405-121-0

KINGDOM WOMAN
978-1-58997-743-3

KINGDOM WOMAN
DEVOTIONAL
978-1-62405-122-7

KINGDOM WOMAN
VIDEO STUDY
978-1-62405-209-5

KINGDOM MARRIAGE
978-1-58997-820-1

KINGDOM MARRIAGE
DEVOTIONAL
978-1-58997-856-0

KINGDOM MARRIAGE
VIDEO STUDY
978-1-58997-834-8

RAISING KINGDOM KIDS
978-1-58997-784-6

RAISING KINGDOM KIDS
DEVOTIONAL
978-1-62405-409-9

RAISING KINGDOM KIDS
VIDEO STUDY
978-1-62405-407-5

KINGDOM FAMILY
DEVOTIONAL
978-1-58997-855-3

CP0845